The
Girl-Son

The
Girl-Son

by Anne E. Neuberger

Carolrhoda Books, Inc./Minneapolis

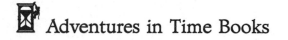

Adventures in Time Books

This book is available in two editions:
Library binding by Carolrhoda Books, Inc.,
  a division of Lerner Publishing Group
Soft cover by First Avenue Editions,
  an imprint of Lerner Publishing Group
241 First Avenue North
Minneapolis, MN 55401 U.S.A.

Website address: www.lernerbooks.com

Library of Congress Cataloging-in-Publication Data

Neuberger, Anne E., 1953–
    The girl-son / by Anne E. Neuberger.
       p.   cm. — (Adventures in time)
    Summary: Based on the life of Induk Pahk, a Korean educator, whose widowed mother disguised her as a boy at the age of eight in order for her to attend school, a choice forbidden to girls in the early twentieth century in that country.
    ISBN 0-87614-846-1 (lib. bdg. : alk. paper)
    ISBN 1-57505-077-3 (pbk. : alk. paper)
    1. Pahk, Induk—Juvenile fiction. [1. Pahk, Indul—Fiction.
2. Korea—Fiction. 3. Sex Role—Fiction.] I. Title. II. Series.
PZ7.N4395Gi 1994
[Fic]—dc20   94-6725

Manufactured in the United States of America
5 6 7 8 9 10 – SB – 06 05 04 03 02 01

To Paul, Nicholas, Peter, and Lucia,
who inspire, delight, sparkle, and shine

Many people helped bring Induk to this book. The author would like to thank all of them, including Dorothy Warner Tribilcock, Mrs. Hyan Sook Han and Jeffrey Mondloh of Children's Home Society of Minnesota, her editor Lisa Kee, Sonja Hur, Kim Duk Rogers, Helen George, Mary Sand, Catherine Vanderhayden-Trescony, Janet Hagberg, and Derek McCarty and Steve Malek and many students and staff members at Saint Mary of the Lake Elementary School, and my family, near and far.

AUTHOR'S NOTE

Once I was reading about the beautiful country of Korea, sometimes called the Land of the Morning Calm. The article focused on a large university and briefly mentioned one of its graduates. As a seven-year-old child, Induk Pahk had been disguised as a boy so she could attend the all-boy village school. There were no schools there for girls.

Over and over again I read those words. How would it feel to be disguised to go to school, I wondered. Was she worried that she might say something that could betray her? Did anyone guess she was really a girl? How long did she dress as a boy?

When she grew up, the article said, she worked hard to start schools in Korea. What happened between pretending to be a boy and founding a school? Perhaps her story was not only interesting, but important as well.

I began searching for clues to Induk's life. Little by little, with the help of people who care about Korea, I was led to two books Induk wrote when she grew up. Her story was indeed interesting and definitely important.

Because Induk wrote about her unusual life, I knew she wanted others to know about it. But the books she wrote were for adults and I felt that younger readers would enjoy getting to know Induk as well.

So, I have written her life story for readers Induk's books might not reach. I have chosen to write it as if Induk herself were here to tell it. And, if you read on, you will find that she tells it in a loud and clear voice.

    —A.E.N.

CHAPTER ONE

The Gift That Changed My Life

In the year 1896, the tiny village of Monyangtul in northern Korea was dotted with cottages thatched with yellow rice straw. The walls of these homes were made of stones, mud, and straw. Windows and doors had *chang ho jee*, or rice paper, covering them.

Inside one of the humble cottages, at the dawn of a September morning, I was born. Instantly, I was a disappointment.

Three sons had been born to my parents. All had died. Now this new baby was a girl.

"Well," my father said. "A girl is better than nothing."

He was a scholarly man, a leader in the community. He taught school in our village. With the blessings of my grandfather, my father had spent his life studying, poring over books of poetry, struggling to perfect his brush strokes for the vast Chinese alphabet. He longed for a son to follow his example.

My mother could not read. She was illiterate, as were most Korean women then. The only way for anyone to earn a living was by farming, and while my father devoted himself to study, my mother worked on the family farm.

On this day, they held me and discussed my signs.

In Korea and China, many people believe that the future of a child can be told by looking at the year, month, day, and hour of his or her birth. Each of these times has a special sign. I was born in the hour of the tiger, the day of the dragon, the month of the rooster, and the year of the monkey. These signs predicted that I would be gifted and powerful. In addition, our village of Monyangtul lay halfway between the mountains, which were considered the tiger's lair, and the sea. Villagers believed this location was the home of the dragon. To be born in the place of the dragon on the day of the dragon was great fortune indeed!

How my parents would have rejoiced at such signs if I had been a boy! But for a girl to be gifted and powerful could be a curse. Girls were expected to be quiet, obedient, gentle.

"If this child shows these signs she'll act clever like a monkey, be as loud as a rooster, powerful as a dragon, and be raging like a tiger! That would be a disgrace!" my father said.

So, carefully, he chose my name: Imduk. It means 'virtuous woman.' He hoped that this name would counteract my powerful signs.

After announcing my name, he sighed, "What a waste of good signs! What a pity she isn't a boy! A boy could have changed the world!"

Mother nodded in agreement.

"Still," he said, "she will lead an extraordinary life."

And I have.

But my father did not live to know this.

When I was six years old, a sickness called cholera swept through Monyangtul. Two-thirds of the townspeople died. My father and brother, born after me, were among the victims.

A few weeks later, one frigid December day, I watched as my mother folded a piece of colorful silk fabric she had woven. I knew she was sad, and I knew she was worried.

In Korea, at the beginning of the twentieth century, a woman alone was nothing. She could not earn money, go to school, or take care of herself when she got old. That is what husbands and sons were for. And Mother had neither. Only me, and I was a girl, as helpless as my mother.

Soon after Father's death, his family met to decide about his property, widow, and child. This could not be the wife's decision. After much discussion, they chose a cousin to inherit my father's estate. Mother and I were free to stay with him, to be dependent on him, but it also meant we were to obey him in all ways, and what we owned now would be his too.

This offer was not an unusual solution, but Mother was not a usual woman. She decided not to accept these terms.

What a crisis this created! Father's family was horrified. Mother's relatives sent word to berate Mother for her stubbornness, and to urge her to reconsider.

"You are a fool!" Father's brother accused. "A woman cannot live alone!"

"You will starve," her brother cautioned. "And so will the child. Think of what you are throwing away!"

Some of Mother's female relatives came together to console and to convince her. One said, "It is a pity the boy did not survive. He would have inherited everything. But at least you still have a daughter."

"How glad I am I have three sons!" another said. "But you have not been so fortunate. Take their offer, dear. It is the best you'll get."

Through all the discussion, Mother held firm to her decision. So when our oxen, rice fields, and lovely home were turned over to the cousin, Mother and I moved to small quarters. We were given only a little money and our clothing.

Her new situation would have left other women frightened or depressed. But not Mother. She used to say, "I do not have trouble. But trouble has difficulties with me!"

In her determined way, she would not let her new life hold her back. Instead of sitting down and weeping at her loss and poverty, she got busy. Immediately she had set up her loom. I loved seeing the exquisite cloth Mother wove. As she folded what she had just taken from the loom, she spoke in a tone that masked her worry.

"When my cousin visited this morning, he told me about a church that is in a village three miles from here. I believe there is a service today. Let's dress and go."

We were Buddhists, as were many Koreans. Mother's cousin had told her of a Christian church. Although Mother, always curious, had questioned him, she still knew very little about this religion.

It was December 25 and bitterly cold. I pulled on my yellow blouse that was padded for winter warmth, my skirt, and my black trousers. We both wore white stockings, also padded, and straw shoes. Mother wore all white—it was a sign that she was mourning for my father and brother. Her clothing was a long skirt over trousers and a short, padded jacket. When she finished winding a kerchief around her head, we set out.

We trudged along a long, desolate road. The snow was deep, the countryside hushed except for the relentless wind. We must have made a sad picture—a broken-hearted, but determined woman leading a little girl. It was clear by her clothing and her manner that my mother was saddened by death, but no one, not even I, knew that Mother was on her way to finding a new life.

My toes were aching and my cheeks stinging when we reached our destination, but I quickly forgot these as curiosity set in. Jubilant sounds seemed to tumble from that small building. Mother often sang at home, but never had I heard such joyful songs as these! The music spilled out of the building, seeming to reach out to us.

I glanced at Mother. She clutched my hand and led me into the building, settling into a space at the back. The church was built in an L shape. On one side sat all the women and girls. Men and boys sat on the other, because it was the custom that after age seven, males were not to sit in the same room as girls and women.

The singing continued, and the woman next to me smiled a welcome. I began to feel a bit warmer, wiggling my toes as they tingled painfully after the cold walk. I tried to join in the song when a now-familiar line was repeated. Mother looked down at me. She seemed pleased that I was participating.

When the song ended, we were all seated. Between the two sections, at the front of the church, was a wooden stand. Later someone told me this was a pulpit. The man called a minister stood at it and began to speak. After the cold walk, the warmth in the church made me sleepy, and I made no attempt to listen to the grown-up talk. But soon I realized he was telling a story. I loved stories and sat up a little straighter, listening intently.

He talked about a mother and father, whose names I could not pronounce. Many years ago, they had gone on a journey, the mother riding a donkey. I was more familiar with oxen, and thought about donkeys until I realized I was missing the story.

This mother and father could not find a place to stay one night. Everything was crowded. I marveled at that. Could no one make room for these people? But again, I was missing the story.

The minister was saying that this woman had a baby that night. There was great singing and rejoicing because of this baby. I was glad. It was always nice when a baby was born, especially a boy. This baby had been a boy. I was glad they were so happy.

I was glad also because another song had begun. We stood again, and I tried to follow along. I had to listen carefully. The song seemed to be about this baby.

When the singing ended, a woman stood up. She said in a loud voice, "Please do not leave yet. There are gifts for the children!"

My heart pounded. My feet felt as if they were made of clay.

"Would the children please come forward?" the minister invited.

Looking at Mother, I received a slight nod, so I joined the children already standing in a circle around the woman. We all glanced at each other nervously. None of us was accustomed to receiving gifts. Many of us did not have all that we needed, much less anything extra.

From the box, the woman pulled out a handkerchief and gave it to the first girl. Next to her was a boy. To him she handed a pencil. Another girl got a handkerchief, another boy, a pencil.

Now I waited a bit more patiently for my new handkerchief. Boys got pencils because they were the ones who learned to read and write. I knew of no girls who went to school. When girls grew up, they were expected to cook and take care of a home. They did not need to read or write to do those jobs.

The smiling woman reached into the box once more as she approached me. In her hand was a pencil!

I put out my hand and felt the thin, hard smoothness of the pencil against my palm. I looked at it closely. It was yellow, the color of sunshine, with a green eraser. I turned it over and over. How straight it was! How glossy!

The minister said, "The pencils come from a store called F. W. Woolworth's, which is far across the sea." I ran my finger along the pencil. I didn't know what this F. W. Woolworth was, or much about the sea. But I had a pencil!

Walking back to where Mother sat, I thought of the children I played with in our village. Most of them still had fathers, and I didn't. But I owned a pencil now, and they did not. It seems a strange comparison but I was young and hurting from the loss of my father. Later, I realized that this pencil, in its own humble way, provided for my life in a way my father never could have.

———— ⊛ ————

On the way home, my straw shoes were making satisfying crunching sounds in the snow, yet I had thoughts only for my pencil. I pleaded with my mother to carry it.

Mother held it firmly. "No. If you drop it in this snow, we'll never find it. You aren't going to waste this pencil, Imduk," she said.

Running to keep up with her, I wondered what use Mother had for this pencil. She walked with her usual vigor, but I sensed more than that. As a child, however, I could not question her. We hurried on in silence.

Early the next morning, I awoke as my mother began moving about the house. Opening one eye, I saw the bleak light of a winter morning.

"Imduk," Mother called, "I have asked a man to come and teach you the alphabet. Get up and dress quickly. He will be here soon."

Shivering, I pulled on my clothes, glancing at Mother wonderingly. Learn the alphabet? I knew no girls who could read!

I heard a soft knock and Mother hurried to the door. She opened it to let in a blast of frosty air and an old man.

He was frail, with a wispy beard the color of new-fallen snow. On his head he wore a tall, narrow stovepipe hat, which he removed upon entering. His long hair was braided and drawn into a knot at the top of his head, held tightly by a horsehair net. This topknot meant he was an educated man. I knew this, for my father, also a scholar, had worn his hair this way. How dignified this man looked in his white scholar's robe!

I wondered where his *podari* was. My father had had one, a small cloth bundle that held the soft, pointed Chinese brush, ink stone, and ink cake. With these my father had spent hours practicing his brush strokes that made up the thousands of characters of the Chinese alphabet.

But this man brought no *podari,* nor any roll of rice paper. Instead, he held a small pad of paper.

I studied his face, a map of wrinkles, and his hands, purpled with veins. He saw me staring.

Though he said nothing, his eyes twinkled at me. I relaxed a bit. Without a word, he sat down on the floor, cross-legged.

The silence among us was broken by a rasping sound. Mother was scraping the end of my blunt pencil with a knife. When it was sharp, she handed it to me, gesturing for me to sit on the floor next to the teacher. Awkwardly, I sat. My first lesson had begun.

Each day for two weeks, my teacher and I bent over the pad of paper, as I labored with my yellow pencil. Mother wove cloth, ever watchful in the background. She did not know if I could actually learn; most people did not think a girl could be taught to read and write. Mother would not waste her money on a teacher if they were right.

But I learned. Fast and well.

At the end of two weeks, my kindly teacher proclaimed me capable of reading and writing Han'gŭl, the Korean alphabet, and quietly took his leave.

"Oh, child!" Mother exclaimed, even giving a little jump for joy. "You can learn just like a boy! You must go to school!"

Holding the little pad now filled with letters, I watched my mother uneasily. It was rare that she showed so much excitement. Rarer still that she should talk so foolishly. Go to school? School was for boys!

Mother did not say how. For a week she was unusually quiet. She seemed deep in thought as she wove and cooked. I asked no questions.

One day Mother was squatting near her cooking pot, pouring rice into it. I liked the soft sh-sh sound the hard rice made as it was poured.

"Imduk, do you remember the tale of the Chinese girl who wanted to be a soldier?" she asked.

"Oh, yes, Mother! Tell it to me again, please?"

"She was young and beautiful but she did not want to live as a girl did. She longed to lead an exciting life. So she quietly left her village, dressed as a soldier, and went to war. Everyone assumed she was a man."

I nodded. I loved this story. Closing my eyes, I was no longer six years old but the woman warrior.

Mother stirred at the fire a bit. "She fought bravely and her fellow soldiers depended on her. Because she was such a good leader, she eventually became a general in the army. She met another general who was a good man. She fell in love with him. After some time, she decided to risk everything and tell him that she was really a woman. He loved her too and later they married."

Opening my eyes, I saw Mother's face and knew she was not finished with her thoughts yet. I waited.

Suddenly she stood up and looked around at the small house. With determination, she said, "I have made a decision. We are going to move to the village of Dukdong, where a relative of mine runs a school for boys. I have thought of a way for you to get an education."

CHAPTER TWO

The Girl-Son

Mother's work-worn hands smoothed the fabric of her black skirt as it lay on the floor. Quickly she began cutting it.

We were in our new home, a single room, in the village of Dukdong. We had planned to live with Mother's brother, but they had quarreled.

He said Mother's idea to educate me was ridiculous. A girl couldn't learn! Where did she get such wild ideas from? No one in their family had such crazy notions!

Stubbornly, Mother clung to her plans and decided to make her own home. This decision took tremendous courage. I knew of no other woman who lived without at least one male relative in her home. By doing this, she was breaking yet another rule of our culture.

"Soon you will have some nice new pants, Imduk. I have made you a pink jacket, just like all the boys wear," Mother explained. Threading a needle with black thread, she began expertly sewing the skirt into pants. Her hands moved methodically. Never did she move unnecessarily.

"A pink jacket?" I asked softly, a little horrified. Pink was for boys.

"Yes. I've made all the arrangements with my relative, Kim Sung-No. He is the principal and has agreed that you may enter his school if I disguise you as a boy."

Disguised as a boy and go to school! I wondered what lay ahead for me. Thoughts of the warrior woman in Mother's story came back to me and I imagined her planning her change from girl to soldier.

I went to bed that night as a girl, but when I awoke, I began my life as a boy.

My red hair ribbons were laid aside. They were for girls. Boys also had long hair, but they braided a black ribbon into it. Mother carefully fixed my hair to look just like a boy's.

This made me think of my little brother, who had died when my father had died. I wondered if Mother also thought of him. I looked into her face. She was peering at my hair, determined that it be exactly right. No, all her thoughts were on me right now.

Next I put on the new pants she had finished late the night before, and the pink jacket.

Now Mother held me at arm's length, her sharp eyes examining me.

"Good," she said with satisfaction. "Now you look just like a boy."

I wiggled a bit, feeling strange in these clothes. Did I really look like a boy?

Mother said solemnly, "You will no longer be called Imduk. You are beginning a new life. For this new life I name you Induk. It means 'benevolence.'"

"Benevolence?"

"Yes. One who does kindnesses. Now that you are Induk, you are my girl-son."

For a moment she paused, and there was silence between us. Then she said briskly, "Now come, Induk. We must leave for the school."

Together we walked through the village, mother and girl-son. She walked proudly and I knew she felt I was just as important as anyone else's boy. I was just as important as her cousin's three sons. I also knew that was a radical idea.

We reached the school quickly, too soon for my comfort. Mother squatted to look intently into my face. I studied her black eyes, understanding the seriousness of her plan.

"You are a boy now," Mother said in a low tone. "Remember your name. If you have been a good boy at school, I will give you all the chicken gizzards you want when you come home."

This was a favorite treat of mine, but first I had to face the school all by myself. Mother could not come with me. She would go back home. Home, where all the girls were.

Gathering all my seven-year-old courage, I entered the school doorway and looked around. The classroom was part of the teacher's home. The floor was made of mud and stone, then covered with oiled paper. As in most Korean homes, because pipes running under the floor were heated by the kitchen stove, the floor was warm.

On this floor sat fifteen boys. Some were little, a bit younger than me. The oldest were around ten years old. Each sat cross-legged and held a Chinese book in his hands, reading aloud. Their voices had a singsong sound. As they read, they swayed to and fro.

The teacher saw me. The principal had assured Mother he would not tell anyone I was a girl, but as the teacher came toward me, I wondered if he could tell I was only pretending to be a boy.

"Come in," he invited. "You may sit at the end of the row."

So I entered this world of boys and men.

Holding my head high as Mother would have, I walked past the seated boys.

Though the chanting of lessons did not stop, I knew

every eye was upon me. I felt my face burning with
embarrassment, and a feeling of fear began welling up
inside of me. Did they guess my secret? Did I really
look like a boy?

The end of the row seemed at the end of the world.
Finally I reached it. I took my place, sitting cross-
legged as the others did. Again I glanced at the
teacher. Did he realize I was a girl? He was walking
toward me. My heart pounded so loudly, I wondered
if the boy sitting next to me could hear it.

But the teacher simply handed me a book called
"One Thousand Characters."

I was now to learn the very complicated language of
China. Highly educated Koreans still used Chinese, a
tradition from long ago.

The teacher said in a kind voice, "You must learn the
first eight characters. Tomorrow you will recite them
aloud and write them without looking at the book."

Opening my book, I looked carefully at the unfamiliar letters. They were not the Han'gŭl letters my
teacher in Monyangtul had taught me.

"If I learned those, I can learn these," I told myself.

And I learned sixteen of them.

It was a good day.

At the end of the school day, I gave a sigh of relief.
No one had noticed all day that I was really a girl! But
as we tumbled out of the classroom, I suddenly realized
that pretending to be a boy in the quiet classroom was

one thing. Being a boy outside was quite another.

The boys began running and shouting playfully. I paused. I had never been allowed to play with boys before.

"Come on, Induk! Race you home!" a boy named Kim Hyun Duk called.

Well, I told myself, I could run! And I chased after him.

When I reached home, Mother greeted me with interest.

"School was good, Mother!" I said. "I am learning the Chinese language. And, Mother—I think I will like being a boy!"

"Here," Mother replied. "I made the chicken gizzards for you."

I knew Mother was proud of me. I imagine she was also very relieved. I had managed to play the part of a boy and had liked it too!

As I relished the chicken gizzards, I realized that Mother had prepared them before I had come home from school. She had expected that I would succeed today. She had believed in me. The chicken tasted even better.

Each day was a little easier. I worked hard, but I enjoyed learning. I felt more comfortable being a boy as each afternoon ended.

Then one morning, the teacher announced it would soon be time for a review. Twice a month, every student recited what he had learned in the past two weeks.

"The student who has learned the most and the one who recites the loudest receives a prize," the teacher reminded us.

I listened, wondering what the prize was. On the way home, however, the boys told me what the teacher had not mentioned.

"I hope you know your lessons well, Induk," Hyun Duk said. "If not, study hard tonight!"

"I do know them," I said confidently.

"Good. Then you are safe," he said.

"Safe?" I asked, becoming uneasy.

"Any student who does not know his lessons is punished," his friend Young Jin explained.

"How?"

"He is whipped across the legs with sticks."

"Everyone watches," Jung Dae, another friend, added.

At home, I studied hard.

The next morning, review day, my heart beat as loudly as it had the first day. I sat cross-legged in my place.

"Induk," called the teacher.

I rose to my feet, a bit wobbly, took a deep breath and began to recite.

The teacher did not look up, but announced, "The prize for the loudest goes to Induk."

Smiling, I sat down. Mother was right. I could

learn just like a boy!

Over the next months, I earned the prize for reciting the loudest many times. Never was I whipped, for I always learned what was expected of me. In three months, I was able to read and write one thousand characters of the Chinese language.

----- ❀ -----

Reading was not the only skill I learned because I went to school with boys. My classmates never suspected I was a girl and welcomed me in their games, which girls would never experience.

With their help, I fashioned a kite and ran over the fields of Dukdong to launch it. The chilly spring air brought roses to my cheeks. I loved the feeling of the taut string tugging in my hand as if the kite were saying, "Let me go! Let me free!"

When the wind was too mild for kite flying, we would gather willow branches, now green and supple, to make whistles from them.

One day, my friend Hyun Duk ran up to me as I walked home from school. "Come on," he invited. "We've found a bird's nest. We're going to get the eggs."

What a strange thing to do, I thought, but out loud I asked, "Where?"

He pointed to a gathering of boys a few houses away. One had climbed the side of a house.

Curious, I joined them. The nest was on the thatched roof. Young Jin was higher up in a tree. He called, "I can't quite reach it."

After he had climbed down, he turned to me. "You try it, Induk. Maybe you can reach it."

I doubted it. I wasn't very tall. But here was my chance to try, and I might never get this chance again. I felt my heart racing as I climbed, carefully placing my foot on a branch and testing it for strength before putting my full weight on it. I had seen Young Jin do this, and I copied his way. I did not want the others to know this was the first time I had tried to get a nest. Reaching the roof, I squatted to keep my balance. As I stretched out my arm to the nest, I wobbled but quickly shifted my weight before I could fall.

My concentration was so strong that the shouts of encouragement from my friends seemed far away. In this new position, I could reach the nest. A bit more of a stretch and my fingers caressed the smoothness of an egg.

Suddenly what I was doing seemed silly. Why take the eggs? But glancing down at the expectant faces below told me I had gotten myself too far into this situation. I couldn't back out now, lest someone suspect I was a girl. Slowly I gathered all three eggs, cushioned them in the pocket of my pink jacket, and lowered myself to the ground.

My friends cheered. Hyun Duk shouted, "Hooray

for Induk!"

The boys gathered around me as I pulled the eggs out of my pocket. Young Jin thumped me on the back with admiration.

"My mother will cook them for us," Jung Dae said. "Let's go!"

I ran off with them, feeling as free as the wind. I could climb trees! And I was good at it!

When spring gave way to the heat of summer, I climbed trees and swung recklessly from ropes tied to them. Hide-and-seek and other games led me to places I had not yet explored.

One scorching day, my friends and I dropped to the ground, panting, after a game of chase. Sweat trickled down my forehead and Hyun Duk was wiping his neck. Young Jin and Jung Dae fanned themselves.

"I'm so hot," Hyun Duk complained.

"Me too," I added, running my hand over my face.

Jung Dae rolled onto his side and propped himself up on his elbow. "I've got an idea!" he announced.

Young Jin seemed to know what he meant. He sat up.

"And it's a great idea! Come on!"

He jumped up, followed by the others. They began running. I scrambled to my feet, calling after them, "Wait! Wait for me!"

I had no idea where we were going, but I did not want to be left out. Despite the heat, I hurried, hoping to soon catch up with the others.

In the distance, the ground sloped. I watched as Young Jin and Jung Dae disappeared down the embankment. I wondered how steeply the ground dropped as I ran along, now gasping for breath.

I reached the hill some minutes after the others, and what I saw brought me to a halt.

Hyun Duk was pulling off his shoes. Jung Dae had stripped to the waist. And Young Jin? I dared not look! For at the bottom of the hill lay a small pond. They were going to swim!

"Come on, slowpoke!" Hyun Duk called cheerfully to me as he too peeled off his shirt.

Immediately I scurried away, fearful that one of the boys would follow me. My heart was pounding, sweat soaked my back, but I ran. I ran all the way back to my house.

Mother looked up from her weaving, surprised at my hasty entrance.

"What's wrong?" she asked.

"The boys—" I panted. "I was playing with the boys—"

Mother stood up and got me a cup of water.

"Here. Drink this. When you are composed, you may tell me."

I sat down, regained my breath, and gratefully drank the water. Then I began again, "I was playing with Hyun Duk and the others until I realized—they were going swimming!"

For a fleeting moment, I saw a look of amusement cross Mother's face. Then she said calmly, "You did right, of course, to come home."

"But what about when I see them again? They'll want to know why I didn't swim with them. Maybe they'll guess why I didn't!"

My voice was high and frantic. Mother resumed her weaving and the familiar motions calmed me.

"Then you must have a good answer for them. Tell them your mother forbids it because it might be dangerous."

"Dangerous, Mother? Don't the boys swim there all the time?" I asked.

Suddenly I realized I had spoken disrespectfully.

Mother looked up. She was not angry. She understood my fear.

"There is always risk in swimming, especially when children are without adults. And, Induk, for you, it would be especially dangerous—dangerous to your education!"

My friends did question me the next day, and I gave them my mother's words. They pooh-poohed the danger, but understood that a mother's orders must be obeyed.

I asked more questions about what my friends' plans were after that, and if swimming was an option, I declined. Someone would say, mockingly, "Induk's mother treats him like a baby—she won't let him swim!"

They would laugh and I would too. What else could I do?

As I walked home, feeling left out of the fun, I knew my mother was getting a reputation for being overly cautious. Little did they know she was taking a great risk with my life, raising me to go against everything these boys believed in. But this was left unsaid. I was relieved my secret was still safe.

Autumn and then winter set in, and my play was unrestricted. I loved the sound of my skates rasping against the unyielding ice, as I glided across the frozen pond. Wild games of chase often caused skaters to sprawl, but I so enjoyed the games, I never complained when it was me.

In January, Hyun Duk told me to meet him at the pond after school. When I got there, he gleefully held up two small wooden poles with ice picks stuck into the ends. On the ice lay a skating board, a rectangle of three boards nailed together to form a seat, with two small runners attached to the bottom.

"Oh, Hyun Duk! What fun you'll have!" I said with envy.

Other boys had these wonderful boards and dashed all over the ice on them, either pushed by friends or scooting along themselves with the help of the poles.

"Grandfather made these for me. And you can have the first ride!"

I looked at him, startled. "But it is yours! You must

have the first ride."

"Go ahead, get on," he laughed. "Grandfather said you were to share this with me."

So I sat on the small board, and Hyun Duk began to push. The runners slid with a shhhh sound. Hyun Duk began to run as fast as he dared on the ice, and I felt as if I were flying. Then he gave me a good hard shove and I sped off alone, whizzing past the bushes on the side of the pond. For a moment, I was totally alone in the world, and whether I were a boy or a girl did not matter at all.

The board gradually lost speed, and as I slowed, I became aware of the silence around me. The winter sky was a gray blue, the tree branches were thin black fingers against it.

Hyun Duk broke my reverie. "Induk!" he shouted. "Use the poles and bring yourself back!"

It was only then that I remembered the sticks on my lap. "Okay, I'll be right there," I called back.

Grasping the poles in each hand, I dug the ends with the picks into the ice ahead of me and pulled. The board slid gracefully back to Hyun Duk, and I jumped off.

"That was great! Thank you!"

"Yes," he answered quickly, and jumped on, eager for his turn. I ran behind, pushing him and then gave him the freeing shove. As he glided away from me, I thought again that being a boy was wonderful. No wonder my father had been disappointed when I was born.

As I progressed in school, Mother watched with pride. She too was working hard. To provide for us, she was now weaving silk and cotton cloth to sell in the village market. She had even begun to raise silkworms and to spin the silk for her weavings. When she had time she studied, determined to learn the Korean alphabet too.

All this I saw. What I didn't see was her concern. I was now eight years old. How much longer could I go on dressed as a boy? Someone was bound to figure out that I was really a girl, and Mother knew that would be the end of my education.

She would not let that happen.

CHAPTER THREE

A Girl Again

Autumn had brought its own special hues. The poplar trees splashed their yellow leaves against the sky. In every courtyard, hundreds of brilliant red peppers lay on straw mats to dry in the sun. Row after row of orange persimmons hung like giants' necklaces, also drying. Winter preparations had begun.

I had been playing a chasing game with my friends. Soon we would be called upon to help with family work, so we played all the harder. Now hot and thirsty despite the chilly air, I broke away from the others to get a drink of water in our house.

As I greedily gulped down a cupful, I realized

Mother was packing our belongings! I halted, wanting to ask her why. But a good child remains silent, waiting for an answer.

She saw me and sat down.

"Induk," Mother said quietly, "I have found a new school for you. There you can continue to study, but you can become a girl again. Imagine—a school for girls! It is in Chinnampo, which is seven miles from here."

Now I could speak. "So we must move?"

Mother nodded. "The school is called Samsung Methodist Mission School for Girls. It is a brand-new school," she explained, then stood up to go on with the packing.

Remaining motionless, I grappled with this news. It was so fun here in Dukdong! I did not want to start all over again. And I wasn't sure that I wanted to be a girl again.

Outside the boys were calling to me. Their laughter and shouts filled the chilly air.

"The school here is good," I ventured.

Mother shrugged, saying simply, "Sooner or later someone will realize you are really a girl. Then you would be forced to leave."

I hadn't thought of that. Pretending I was a boy had become so easy. Glancing out the door where the boys were scuffling and teasing each other, I imagined someone announcing that I was a girl.

The embarrassment! The shame!

But why? Why was it wrong to be a girl? I learned
as well as the boys did—better than some of them!
Looking at Mother as she folded the blues and greens
of her weavings, I felt she should be proud, not
ashamed of who she was.

Mother looked up from her work. Her voice was a
bit sharp. "What is it?"

"I don't understand," I said. "I learn as well as the
boys do. Why can't I go to school here as a girl?"

She sighed, but she was not angry with me. Again
she sat down. Because a far away look came over her
face, I knew a story was coming. It would not be a
happy one.

"When I was your age, I wondered why I couldn't
do as my brothers did. I wanted to go to school too,"
she said.

She was not speaking to me, but to herself. "But
that is the way it's been for many, many years. Men
rule, they run the country, so they are the ones educated. It is hard, very hard to change such things."

Mother fell silent.

My friends called to me impatiently. I made no move
toward the door. Abruptly Mother stood up.

"This new school is one chance to change that, at
least for you," she said in a final tone. "Now run and
play. I must pack."

There was no use to speak of it again. Mother had decided. I must leave Dukdong and become a girl again.

I did not like this turn of events. Dragging my feet, I scuffed toward the door and paused to look at my mother. Her shoulders were set determinedly as she collected our cooking pots. At that moment I understood my mother would stop at nothing to educate me.

—— ❀ ——

A few days later, we left our little home at dawn. Mother hoisted her *jee-geh,* the A-framed pack, onto her back. In it were all our possessions. I trotted along beside her, as we passed the devil posts, tall stakes of wood on which villagers had carved frightening faces, hoping to fend off evil spirits that brought hunger and sickness. I paused to study them. The wood on two had weathered to a soft gray, but a third, much newer, still retained its light reddish brown color. On all three, the eyes were large and blank, but they seemed to stare menacingly at me. The noses were long and ended at the wide, expressionless mouths.

I didn't think these posts worked. My father and brother had died of sickness, and my mother and I were sometimes hungry. I was glad to leave them behind, and I had to hurry to catch up with Mother, whose fast pace had left me alone with the posts.

In a few hours, my friends would be walking this same road to school, but they would be walking without me. Other times, they would be climbing trees, flying kites, and making whistles without me. Winter would come, and they would skate without me.

My thoughts ran to Hyun Duk. He had always been so kind to me. He would wonder why I was not at school today. Perhaps he would stop by our house and find it empty. I would never see him again. Perhaps if he did see me, he would not even know me, for today I wore my girl clothing. My black hair was again braided with the red ribbon. Of course, if I did ever see Hyun Duk again, we could never be friends. I was a girl now, and boys and girls could not play together. The only thing that remained the same from yesterday was my name: I would keep Induk.

On the way, in another village, we saw a girl my age carrying water, and boys also my age going to school. I looked at them with interest. Glancing at Mother, I knew she was thinking of the differences in their lives. She began walking faster. I had to run to keep up with her.

Mother was silent for most of the walk. Then from a field, a little dog approached us. I was surprised when Mother stopped, stooped down and began petting the animal. She talked to it in soothing tones. I watched, fascinated as the dog looked up at her with trusting eyes. After several minutes, Mother stood up, gave the dog one last pat, and we started off, though Mother seemed reluctant to leave the dog behind. It walked with us several yards before heading back to the field.

"That dog makes me think of the dog I had when your father and I were married," she said.

"What was its name?" I asked, hoping for a story.

"Bok-Suree."

"Blessed Dog?" I asked.

"Yes," she said. "She was little and brown. She went with me everywhere—when I drew water from the well, Bok-Suree was with me. When I was hoeing and picking the cotton in the fields, she came too. When I was about to be married, I wanted to bring Bok-Suree with me to your father's house."

"Did you?"

Mother laughed. I sensed her mind was no longer present to me but back in a younger time.

"My mother said of course I could not take the dog with me. Most people don't keep dogs as pets, and she was afraid your father's family would object."

"Did you ever see your dog after you were married?" I asked.

Again she laughed. "Yes, I certainly did! After the wedding, we spent two nights with my family before moving to your father's family home. When we were leaving my home, my family had to hold Bok-Suree back. She barked and barked—I did feel bad. But soon we arrived at your father's house, and I had to settle into my new life. At supper time, I was busy getting a meal ready. Someone noticed a strange dog wandering around the house. Your grandmother, my new mother-in-law, thought the dog looked weary and hungry. She let it in for something to eat. I turned to look—there was Bok-Suree! She leaped on me, whimpering, panting, and licking me all over my face! I began crying!"

I smiled at the thought of my mother crying over a dog. "Did you get to keep Bok-Suree?"

"Yes, your grandmother immediately said Bok-Suree was to stay. The dog had traveled ten miles to find me!"

We fell silent again, but there was a lightness and warmth to our silence. I was glad Mother had told me that story.

Soon we reached Chinnampo. It was a village like the others we had passed. High on a hill, beyond the cluster of thatched cottages, stood Samsung Methodist Mission School for Girls.

Mother slipped the *jee-geh* off when we reached the top of the hill.

"Look, child," she said, panting a bit after the steep climb. She pointed below to the opposite side of the hill. "The Yellow Sea."

For several minutes, Mother and I gazed at the body of water that separated Korea from China. I did not know that I would stand on this spot many times to see this beauty. I did not know that I would stand there alone.

"Wait with the pack. I will go inside and speak with the principal," Mother directed.

Now that we were miles from my old school, curiosity about this new place set in. I would meet girls! Would they like me? What games would we play? Would Mother and I live near some of my new friends?

When Mother appeared in the doorway, my excitement sunk. Her face was set in an unreadable way. I knew that could mean trouble. What had happened? Had the school refused me?

She said simply, "There is a room for you to sleep in. Before we go to it, we must get you a few things."

I did not understand. A room here for Mother and me? We were to live at the school? How strange! And why would Mother have to buy me anything? There was so little money.

"Come along," she said briskly, settling the *jee-geh* on her back once again. Then she paused, sensing my confusion.

"You will live at the school. They've been kind enough to give you an empty space. You will cook for yourself, so we must get you a cooking pot."

The awful truth was beginning to seep in.

"I will live at the school?" I asked. "With you?"

"No, just you."

There was now a throbbing in my chest. Where would my mother be?

I was too fearful to ask. Instead, I said, "Do the other girls stay at the school too?"

"No, you will be the only one. The others live at

home and come to school each day."

Now I was flooded with panic. "Why can't I?"

Mother's voice was very even. "Because there won't be any home for you to come to. We had barely enough to eat in Dukdong. In order for me to make a little more money, I've decided to become a peddler. If I can travel from village to village, I think I can sell my weavings. I'll take needles and thread and stop at houses to make clothing for children from my cloth."

"In the winter?" I asked. "Where will you be when you cannot travel?"

"I will live with your uncle. There I can weave for my next travels."

"And I can live with you then?"

"Uncle's house is too far away for you to live there and attend school. I will see you at every school vacation."

Mother turned and began the trek down the hill, but I stood perfectly still. I wanted to go to school, but not this badly! I'd rather carry water, like the girl we had seen earlier, than live alone! How I wanted to cry, to beg her to change her mind, but a child must not be so bold. I knew, too, that my mother was a very determined woman. I could not have changed her mind even if I had been permitted to speak to her about her decision.

As Mother was now partly down the hill, I scurried after her. When I caught up, she said firmly, "From now on, you must cook your own rice. We cannot be one another's servants."

Mother often spoke abruptly and never for long. She became silent now. She expected me to be the same.

My mind was moving as quickly as my legs now. Everything had changed so fast! Just last night, I had gone to bed as a boy, in my old home. Now I was a girl, and tonight I would be sleeping at the new school, without my mother!

In the market, Mother chose a cooking kettle, a few dishes, a spoon, and chopsticks. Then she purchased some rice and a few vegetables. I watched as she counted her coins carefully. That was most of the money she had in the world.

We headed once again to the hill. The kettle filled with the spoon and dishes was burdensome. As it banged against my legs, I knew I should be grateful for these new things, but they only spoke to me of my mother's leaving. Each step was taking me closer to the school and the time when she would be gone.

Mother easily found the room I was to stay in when we arrived back at school. It was a bare little space. My quilt, cooking utensils, and few clothes did little to fill it. It took only moments to unpack. Then I was moved in, and Mother could go.

Again I felt the throbbing in my chest. My stomach felt queasy.

Mother hugged me and said in a quiet, firm voice, "Even though you are a girl again, I am still as proud

of you as any son. You will always be my girl-son.
Study hard. I'll do all I can so you can study. I'll see
you as often as possible."

And then she was gone.

My room was still. I spread my quilt on the floor,
wondering when I'd see my mother again. It seemed
as though I were the only person in the whole world.

In Korea, families lived closely. Grandparents, parents, children, even aunts and uncles lived in small
houses together. That Mother and I had lived without
extended family had been very rare. Now I was completely alone. I had never been alone before.

What now? I had walked over seven miles that day,
so I was hungry. I began to make my dinner early.
This was my first attempt at cooking.

Mother had found an old kerosene can for my stove.
In fine weather, I was to cook out in the courtyard. In
winter, I could use the teachers' kitchen. At home, in
Dukdong, everyone kept a tiny fire, called a seed fire,
going all the time, coaxing it into a bigger fire at cooking times. If it went out, we went to a neighbor's to
"borrow" a small flame on a bunch of straw. Today
Mother had set up the sticks to become the seed fire
and then secured a bit of fire for me by stopping in the
teacher's kitchen. That was smoldering now, but it
was up to me to kindle it into a flame for cooking.

I had not been allowed to build fires often, so I was
nervous as I built up some sticks over the burning

coals. I relaxed a bit when a cheerful little blaze was burning and my fingers were not.

Now I poured some rice into the new pot and added as much water as I thought Mother would have. Putting the lid on the pot, I sat back to wait for my dinner.

Soon a burning smell filled the air around me. Hastily I took the lid off the pot. All the water had been absorbed and the rice was scorched to the bottom of the pot! Hurriedly, I put out the fire, carefully setting aside a few coals. With my spoon I scraped some of the rice out and tasted it. Pooh! It tasted awful! I dumped the rice out, hoping the birds would want it. What a waste of precious food!

"I can't do this!" I wailed to myself.

Why did my mother leave me to care for myself? I couldn't cook! I was only eight years old. I needed her!

But this kind of thinking wasn't going to feed me, and I was very hungry. Fighting back tears, I scraped the pot clean, then washed it. Determined not to waste any more rice, I built a very small fire.

"This time it won't burn!" I thought as I carefully measured the rice and water into the pot.

The rice did not burn. It did not cook either. Fifteen minutes went by, then a half hour. I waited, but finally, almost dizzy with hunger, I peeked into the pot.

The rice was firm, still unable to be eaten, the water unabsorbed!

This was too much! I wanted my mother! Tears

slipped down my cheeks. I longed to be back in Dukdong, in my old school, living with my mother, who could cook rice!

But of course the only thing to do was to build up the fire if I was ever going to eat tonight. I did so, being careful to keep it smaller than the first fire.

After a time, I checked the rice. It was perfect! And delicious. My chopsticks moved quickly from bowl to mouth. I felt so much better now that I admired the beauty of the new bowl and felt proud of having cooked my own dinner.

When the darkness came on, however, and I lay in my new room by myself, all the happy feelings fled. The autumn wind outside was brisk, and a tree near my window caused a shadowy dance on the walls.

I thought about my mother. Was she missing me tonight? I wanted her to tuck my quilt up to my chin.

"Think about school," I told myself, trying not to cry.

But that only made me nervous. What would the girls be like? And the teachers? What subjects did they study here? I remembered my old school, my old friends.

I wondered if I'd even like being a girl again.

The wind made a whooshing sound against the building. I pulled the blanket over my head. I wished my mother were sleeping nearby. I wondered where she was sleeping tonight.

It was a long, long time before I slept.

—— ❇ ——

When the sun shone in my window, I woke with a start. Where was I?

Samsung Methodist Mission School for Girls!

I was up in a flash, gobbling down the cold rice left over from last night's dinner. Then I dressed. It was difficult to braid my hair without Mother's help. Without Mother. A wave of loneliness swept over me. Was she thinking of me this morning?

Outside my room I heard voices and footsteps. Taking a deep breath, I stepped out to meet my new life.

The next few hours were a blur of activity. I met the nineteen other students—the girls! Isabel Chang, the principal and also a teacher, welcomed me warmly and assigned a desk to me. It felt good to be learning again, and for the daytime at least, I could forget I was the only student living by myself and concentrate on classes. After a few days, life had a routine.

Because this was a religious school, each day we studied the Bible. Silently we memorized small parts, to be tested the following day. Each night, in my quiet room, I recited my passages out loud. The kerosene lamp cast a warmth and the words were comforting. I felt safe here, and I knew my mother loved me.

A new subject for me was math, or arithmetic, as it was called. I had not studied this in Dukdong. I resumed my study of the Chinese language, taught by another teacher, a man named Lee Kun-Wo. My favorite was singing class. All my bottled up feelings came tumbling out as I joined the other girls in song.

On the first day, I had discovered something wondrous in the corner of the classroom. It was a large wooden box, which had black and white rectangles that lay on one part of it. I was puzzling about it when Miss Chang approached it, announcing it was singing time.

To my amazement, she sat down at it, and when her fingers gently touched those rectangles, beautiful music came out! She seemed to move her feet too, but the music came from the movement of her fingers and those rectangles. She noticed my astonishment.

"This is called an organ, Induk," she said. "A reed organ. Do you like its sound?"

I could only nod and stare. What beauty! And every day, this organ was part of our singing. It filled me with joy each time.

When the days were done, the other girls skipped home, their books bouncing inside large kerchiefs tied around their waists. I always watched them go. Sometimes they complained among themselves that boys and other villagers made fun of them for going to school. They dreaded the taunts of the boys, which puzzled me. What was there about boys to be afraid of? It was girls I wondered about. With envy, I stood on the hill, seeing them go off in twos and threes.

When they left, the school was quiet, and my long evening began.

I took to gazing out onto the Yellow Sea every day, for I loved watching the large ships moving gracefully, like giant swans in the water. Plumes of smoke rose from each ship. Tracing these with my finger, I mused, "Where is this one going? And that one? What is beyond the Yellow Sea?"

As the school year progressed, I learned what was beyond the sea. As my Chinese improved, I began reading books. I read about places and people I never knew existed.

One day I read about a man named Christopher Columbus. That was the first I had heard of the Americas. I read about the kings of countries called Britain and Italy, who would not give Columbus aid for his travels. Soon, I learned, the queen of Spain agreed to help him. My book said Columbus then thanked Queen Isabella for her benevolence. That word, written in Chinese, leaped out at me. I read it over and over. It used the same characters that I used to write my name! I remembered that long-ago day in Dukdong when Mother had renamed me. She had said that Induk meant "benevolence," or one who does kindnesses. And here in this textbook was my name, used to describe the queen of Spain who had granted Columbus help for his explorations! I felt important. I vowed to live up to my name. And I vowed that

someday, I would see some of these places I was reading about.

Soon after this discovery, a visitor came to our school
and gave us a firsthand account of another place I had
never heard of. He was a young Korean man who had
recently returned from a place called Hawaii. He spoke
of blue waters surrounding islands of flowers and fruit
so delicious it melted in the mouth.

All too soon his talk was over. I wanted to hear
more! Closing my eyes, I found myself vowing again:
someday, I would go there!

——— ❀ ———

A few months into the school year, I was lying in my
room one night and thinking of my mother, as I often
did before I slept.

Two years before, my father and brother had died.
We had left two villages behind since then. Rarely did
we see other family members. Mother was the only
person who had always been there for me. I wanted to
be with her.

She had let the school principal know approximately
where she would be in case of an emergency. Now she
was only about four miles away.

Four miles! I could easily walk that distance! A
plan began to form. I would surprise her with a visit.
As there were no classes, I could go the next day.

At dawn, I pulled on my straw shoes and began the walk. My legs actually felt light from excitement. The wind seemed to push me. Had I been any more excited, I might have flown!

On the road, I met a peddler carrying his wares on his back, the way Mother did. I imagined her now, hoisting her heavy *jee-geh* onto her back, sewing for other families while living away from her only child, all so I could go to school. I walked even more quickly.

Soon the village was in sight, and I began to run. By asking around, I had no difficulty locating the house where my mother was staying.

There she was.

In Korea, we often announce our arrival by clearing our throats. I did so now.

She looked up from the piece of cotton she was sewing. For a brief moment I saw surprise, then delight on her face. Then it closed to me. She turned her back and would not look at me.

"I'm doing all I can to provide for you. You must do your part by studying. Go back to school, Induk," she said quietly.

My excitement burst like a balloon hitting a tree branch. I was confused, almost frightened. My mother would not welcome me? I could not understand. She must!

But Mother continued to sew, her back toward me. She said no more.

Tears slipped down my cheeks. I wanted to run to

her, put my arms around her. But what if she still refused me? Then it would be even worse than it was
now. I hesitated for a moment, but since my mother
had taught me never to question her decisions, there
was nothing to do but obey her.

Taking one last look at her back, I left the house.

The four miles back to Samsung were like one hundred. Leaving the village behind, I walked in great be-
wilderment. Why? Why would Mother not see me?
Had I done something wrong?

By the time I reached Samsung, my eyes ached from
crying, but I had come to accept that Mother wanted
me to stay at Samsung. And despite my pain, I knew
that she loved me.

In my room, I looked at my books and my little rice
kettle, gifts from my mother. Exhausted, I lay down
on my quilt and slept.

It would be years before I understood that my
mother refused to welcome me because she was afraid
if she did, I'd leave school often to find her, or worse,
ask to stay with her. She felt she must discourage this
right away.

It would be even longer before I understood that the
pain I felt that day was but a fraction of what Mother felt.

———— ❀ ————

In a way, it was good, this incident with Mother.

Now I saw Samsung as my only home and I better accepted life there.

I loved to learn. The days in the classroom were challenging and exciting. And, alone in my room, I had nothing to do but study. I progressed well.

There was something else I needed to learn, however, and that was how to be a girl! In Dukdong I had learned games that only boys could play, and sometimes when all the girls had gone home for the day, I climbed a tree. I did not want to completely give up boys' ways. However, I was always careful to not let on about my knowledge because I wanted to be accepted by the girls. I missed the fun of playing with friends.

Gradually the other girls began to accept me and I them. During the Korean New Year celebration, I was invited to a family's home. I watched, fascinated, as a few of my classmates gathered near the wall that surrounded the house. One girl placed a long board across a straw mat that had been rolled up, to form a seesaw. Then she stepped onto one end of the board and her friend jumped onto the other. When the friend's weight hit the board, the first girl was pushed several feet into the air. She could see over the wall for a few seconds.

The other girls laughed and shouted, "What do you see?"

"Nothing yet," she giggled as she landed.

Each girl got several chances to jump and the others

always asked the same question.

I did not know what they were looking for, but I wanted to join the jumping. One girl, Yun Sim-Sung, noticed me watching.

"Come on, Induk!" she called. "Come jump with us."

Gladly I entered the circle. When it was my turn, I flew into the air. It was a wonderful feeling of lightness, but somehow I thought I'd left my stomach behind!

Over the wall, I saw a few boys approaching.

I landed, my feet tingling.

"What did you see?" came the chorus.

"Oh, some boys. They were coming this way," I said casually.

I was unprepared for the explosion of giggles and shrieks that followed my answer. Then there were whispers. Who could be next to jump? I didn't understand all this fuss.

Soon we heard the boys outside the wall. One brave girl jumped, and to the shrieks and giggles on our side came shouts from the boys.

She came down, reporting excitedly, "There are three of them—about our age!"

More giggles. The boys called to us. Another girl jumped. More shrieks, more shouts.

Finally, I understood. As boys and girls could not play together, and rarely talked with each other, these games were one of the few ways they even saw each other.

I was lucky, I realized, to have had my "boy year" in Dukdong.

In the summer, Sim-Sung asked me to spend a night at her house. That afternoon, we gathered flowers called *Pong Sun Wha*.

It was fun being with her, and the flowers were pretty. But Sim-Sung was not gathering them to make a bouquet. She put the blossoms into a bowl, pouring a powder over them. As she mixed, she pounded on the flower petals with a spoon.

"What is that powder?" I asked, fascinated. "Why are you doing this?"

"Haven't you done this before, Induk?" she asked, a bit perplexed by my ignorance. She pounded steadily. "The powder is called *pakban*. When it is mixed with the flowers, it makes a fingernail dye."

Before we went to sleep, Sim-Sung painted my nails with the dye and wrapped each nail with *Pong Sun Wha* leaves. She did not paint my index fingers.

"You forgot these," I said, wiggling them in the air.

"No. We always leave them undyed," Sim-Sung replied.

"Why?"

She chuckled a little before answering. "Because we always do. Our mothers always did, their mothers always did. That's all! I can do your big toes, too, if you want."

"Because we always do, and our mothers always

did?" I teased, lying back and wiggling my toes in the air.

Again she laughed. "Yes, Induk! But when you get married, you can paint only the last two fingers. And when you're older, like our mothers are, you paint only the little fingers."

I looked at my fingers encased in leaves. They looked so funny! Then I realized Sim-Sung was looking at me expectantly.

"Do you want me to paint your nails—all but the index fingers?" I asked.

Sim-Sung smiled and nodded.

With hands clumsy with the unfamiliar feeling of leaves on my fingertips, I painted Sim-Sung's nails.

"Wait and see!" she said as we drifted off to sleep.

In the morning, we pulled off the leaves. Our nails were a beautiful red.

At breakfast, Sim-Sung's mother admired our hands.

"Remember," she said. "If your nails keep the red coloring till the first snow falls, you will have good luck!"

I smiled. I already had good luck—a friend like Sim-Sung, and a good school. I admired my nails all the way back to Samsung.

———— ⊛ ————

I spent four years at Samsung Methodist Mission School for Girls. During school vacations, Mother and

I spent weeks together. Those were happy, warm times. She had learned the Korean alphabet, Han'gŭl, so she could read now too. I was as proud of her as she was of me.

When I returned to school I missed her deeply, but the routine of school was comforting. How I loved to learn!

Now I was twelve years old. The first class of Sam-sung was ready for graduation. Sim-Sung and I were the only ones in the class. We were both to give a speech.

The speech teacher had assigned me the topic, "From the seed of suffering springs joy," an idea from the Bible. After I had labored to write the speech, I read it to the teacher.

The other students had gone home for the day. The classroom was hushed when I finished reading. I sat down.

"Induk, you mumble! Why speak at all if the audience cannot understand you?" the teacher commanded. "You will not be speaking in a classroom, but a large room filled with people. With that in mind, read it again."

I stood and began reading.

"Chin up! You are drooping!" she roared like a lion at me.

I tried again, a bit unnerved. The teacher in Dukdong had always complimented me on my ability to speak. But this teacher seemed to think I could do better. I was not as sure.

"You will drop your words on the floor! Louder!

And pronounce everything clearly!"

Over and over and over again I recited that speech. At last I heard the welcome words, "That's better."

The day of graduation arrived. Sim-Sung and I sat on the stage, wearing new white dresses. Pots of red azaleas surrounded us. I looked out into the crowd. There were at least two hundred people, all looking at Sim-Sung and me!

My mouth went dry. Which shook more, my hands or knees? When I stood to speak, my eyes caught those of my speech teacher. She looked back at me, full of confidence. I took a deep breath.

In a loud, clear voice, I began, "From the seed of suffering..."

When I finished, the audience broke into wild applause! I stood there to accept the praise, but felt greatly embarrassed. I scanned the people in the front rows. There was Mother, looking at me with pride and love.

I wanted to jump and shout to her, "Your girl-son did it!" But instead, I stood respectfully on the stage.

Suddenly I realized that this was really over. I was graduating from Samsung! What now? I didn't want to stop learning. But higher education meant money and Mother had so little. I did not even know if there were any high schools for girls.

When the applause was over, I threaded my way through the crowd of well-wishers to find Mother. We met and embraced. As she held me in her arms, I

thought back to the time when she had no way of getting me into a school, just because I was a girl.

There would be a way this time too.

CHAPTER FOUR

Ewha High School's Newest Student

 "Mother!" I called, running into my uncle's home, where I was staying with Mother a few weeks after graduation. "Remember my friend Sim-Sung? I have just received a letter from her. She wrote that there is a girls high school in Seoul! She is going to go there now that she's graduated from Samsung. I want to go too!"

Mother looked thoughtful.

"Seoul! That is a long way from here," she said. "If you want to go, I will help you as much as I can, but you would need money for tuition, room, and board!"

I shook my head, catching my long black hair with

my fingers. "Sim-Sung said I could just go with her if I can afford the travel money."

"Oh, it cannot be as simple as that, Induk," Mother said doubtfully, but I knew she was as excited as I was.

"Sim-Sung assured me it was! The school's name is Ewha. It is a mission school like Samsung, and it is free!"

Mother remained silent for a moment and her eyes searched my face. This time, I was the determined one. Much had changed since that miserable day when a little girl left school to find her mother.

"All right. I will help you with the transportation money," Mother said with characteristic seriousness. Then she smiled, "You will get a higher education! You will be a scholar, just like your father! How proud I was of him."

I knew that was her way of telling me she was proud of me. We embraced. I was still her girl-son.

———— ✿ ————

One morning in early September, I began my journey to Seoul. Traveling with me were Mother, Sim-Sung, and her father. The nearest place to catch a train for the great city of Seoul was the city of Pyong-yang, forty miles away. Sim-Sung's father put our belongings on his back, and we started our walk.

This was not the first time I had walked forty miles.

But despite her father's help, the day seemed unending. We passed miles of farm fields, countless farmers bending over their work. Each cottage looked like the last one. At first Sim-Sung and I chatted, but eventually, silence fell upon us as we tired. Sim-Sung's father kept the pace. Mother, usually quiet, gave us instructions for our new life ahead.

Footsore and weary, we finally reached Pyongyang the following day and stayed the night at an inn, a first for me.

The next morning, we headed for the train station. In the distance we could hear the South Manchurian Express coming from Antung. I had never been near a train, much less ridden on one. I clutched my ticket, which cost one *won*. I could travel for half-fare because of my age. In a few days I would be thirteen and would have to pay full fare. Suddenly the train neared the station, smoking like a fearsome dragon. Soon I would climb onto this dragon and be whisked away.

Mother stood on the platform. She did not cry, but smiled and gave me one final instruction, "Induk, you are my girl-son. Study hard and believe in yourself. And be brave."

Sim-Sung and I boarded the train, our legs feeling unsure on this swift-moving beast. Sitting by the window, I waved to Mother as the train began to inch along and then gradually build up speed and power.

I was finally on my way to high school! Glancing at

Sim-Sung, I realized she was looking at me. We giggled. I shivered with excitement, trying to settle in for the long ride. I did not think about the fact that no one at the school had ever heard of me, much less knew I was coming.

As we left Pyongyang behind, gray clouds were gathering in the sky above the Korean countryside. I gazed out the window at the mountains shrouded in gray. A gentle rain began to fall. I thought of Mother. I closed my eyes, afraid I might cry. Lulled by the rocking motion of the train, I began thinking about my father.

He, too, had traveled to Seoul as a scholar. He had the honor of taking the national examinations, in hopes of securing a government job. My father had walked the nearly two hundred miles to Seoul and despite years of study, had failed the extremely difficult tests. He was preparing to take them again when the government discontinued this practice.

I wondered what he would think of his little Imduk now. He had never known me as Induk. What name would he give me now, if he could see me traveling to Seoul to go to high school? Perhaps "Flying Dragon."

Now I felt calmer and opened my eyes. I wondered what the new school would be like.

The train slowed and stopped at Kaesong. Passengers got off, new ones got on. Sim-Sung and I amused ourselves by watching the newcomers settle in. Their speech sounded a little different from what I was used to.

A woman sat down near us, her hair twisted into a bun, which she had pinned at the nape of her neck. I looked around at other women arriving. All had this little bun. None of them wore their hair like Mother or other women of my villages, who braided their hair, wrapping it around their heads. What other differences would I see as I approached Seoul?

Hours later, night was coming on and the rain had increased to a steady downpour. The train was approaching the large city of Seoul.

I pressed my face against the window, not wanting to miss a thing. Pyongyang was the largest place I had ever been in. There had been more houses than I could count. Here, in Seoul, the houses and buildings went on endlessly. And though it was dark, there were lights everywhere! I turned to Sim-Sung.

She too was peering out the window. With enthusiasm she said, "Aren't the lights pretty? They are electric."

Sim-Sung had been to Seoul once before.

I was about to question her about this word *electric,* but each moment there were new wonders.

"Look!" Sim-Sung exclaimed, pointing to a large, ornate building in the distance. "There is Duksoo Palace! It once belonged to a great king and queen. She gave our school the name Ewha. It means 'pear blossom'."

The train had begun to slow down, but my heart sped up. When the train reached the station, we stood up on unsteady legs, gathering our bags. Once off, we met two older girls, who were also bound for Ewha High School.

I looked around at the huge station. Confusion flooded me. How far were we from Ewha?

"Nothing like a little walk in the rain!" one of the girls said cheerfully. "It's just a few miles."

We gathered up our bundles as the rain poured steadily down. I hugged my quilt, a gift from my mother, trying to keep it as dry as possible. It was also a comfort as I walked through this big, confusing place.

The four of us hurried through the streets of Seoul. Sim-Sung and the two older girls chatted despite the rain. They seemed happy to be on their way to school. I did not join the conversation because I was too busy taking in the sights of the great city. The electrical lights were magical, the large buildings astounding! I wished Mother were here with me to share in this.

Finally, a grand, two-storied red brick building was within sight.

"Welcome to Ewha, Induk!" one of the older girls said to me.

We sped up and soon were hurrying up steps to a veranda to escape the rain. When we stopped, I looked about in awe. Yes, I had arrived at Ewha High School!

"Here we are at last!" said the oldest girl, setting her bags down. "Beautiful, isn't it? Did you know that when this school started, about one hundred years ago, there was only one student! This is the very first school for girls in all of Korea!"

Fascinated, I was about to ask more questions, but Sim-Sung seemed anxious. "We better tell the principal we've arrived," she urged, wiping a strand of wet hair from her eyes. "Induk, will you wait here with our bags?"

I nodded and the others passed through the front door. Suddenly, I felt very alone in this towering city, so unlike the villages of home. Those lights seemed to be everywhere! I wondered if someday I could visit the palace Sim-Sung had pointed out. There was so much to learn about here! Yes, I might be lonely at times, but I was glad I had come!

The door opened and Sim-Sung came toward me. I thought she looked worried, but she said only, "Come with me."

Gathering up her baggage, she added, "Miss Frey told me that you are to sleep in my room. Tomorrow you and I must meet with her."

"Miss Frey? Is she the principal?" I asked, my bag banging against my legs as I followed Sim-Sung.

"Yes. You'll have to tell her why you came here."

"That's easy!" I said with a laugh. "I want to get a high school education."

Sim-Sung shifted her bag from one hand to the other. "It might not be that simple," she said.

An uneasy feeling began to creep into my stomach.

I wanted to ask Sim-Sung what she meant, but we had approached another two-story building and I followed Sim-Sung inside.

There was a large staircase. I marveled as I climbed it. I had never climbed indoor steps before!

Down a long corridor we trudged, excitement wearing thin now, bags seeming heavier. Sim-Sung stopped at room number three, and said, "Here we are."

She opened the door and we peered in. The room had a stone floor, covered with oil paper. A chest of drawers, a low desk, a broom and dust pan, a polishing cloth, and a pail furnished the room. In the center of the ceiling a light glowed.

For a moment, I gazed up at the fixture in the ceiling, figuring this must be one of those electric lights.

Tired after our lengthy travels, we changed out of our wet clothing and quickly made up our beds on the floor. I unrolled the blue quilt. It was surprisingly dry on the inside. Soon after we were both nestled into our quilts, the light darkened.

"What happened?" I cried out. Used to the gentle flicker of oil lamps at home, I felt plunged into the darkness. I sat up, more curious than frightened.

Sim-Sung laughed. "There is a master switch in the office where all the lights can be turned off," she explained. "Did you know those lights were invented by a man named Thomas Edison in a country called the United States?"

I lay back down. "Oh. I've read about that place. I would like to go there."

"It is very far away," Sim-Sung said drowsily. "Good night, Induk."

I wished her a good night, grateful for all her help. But as the silence and the darkness settled over me, I felt tension from my long journey seep in. I wondered what Sim-Sung had meant when she had said that talking with the principal might not be easy. Then, thoughts of home returned to me. I wanted my mother.

Struggling to keep from crying, I recalled Mother's words. Snuggling down further into my blue quilt, I repeated them over and over, "Be brave! Be brave!"

———— ⊛ ————

The autumn sun warmed my face. I awoke to find myself in room number three at Ewha High School, the soft quilt enfolding me. Sim-Sung was sitting up.

She laughed a bit as she greeted me, "Good morning! You look as if you'd forgotten where you were!"

Grinning back at her I admitted, "Yes, I guess I had."

"We'd better dress and go see Miss Frey. She told me we were to come first thing in the morning."

"Oh yes," I said, the butterflies in my stomach starting up again. Trying to sound casual, I asked, "Is she American?"

"Yes," Sim-Sung answered, pulling on her shoes. "Come on. We'd better hurry."

Soon we were climbing the steps of the large brick building where I had waited last night. I intended to concentrate on how to get to the principal's office, but curiosity got the better of me and I was glancing into every room and hallway we encountered before we reached the main office.

Together we sat on a bench, waiting to be called. Sim-Sung clasped and unclasped her hands. I remained silent, but the uneasy feeling had returned. In Chinnampo, coming here to Ewha had seemed like such a wonderful idea. Now it seemed daring. Maybe even foolish. I longed to ask Sim-Sung if she regretted bringing me here, but I was afraid of her answer.

"Miss Frey will see you now, girls," a voice said.

I did not even look to see who had called us. Now my stomach felt like a clenched fist. "Be brave," I told myself.

Miss Frey sat behind a bulky desk. For a moment, I stared at her, unaccustomed as I was to blonde hair and blue eyes. And she was so tall!

Then I realized my disrespectful behavior, and quickly lowered my eyes.

Sim-Sung stepped forward. In a small but steady voice, she said, "Miss Frey, this is Induk Pahk. She went to Samsung School with me. We graduated in the same class. I asked her to come with me to Seoul so she could also get a high school education."

Miss Frey's eyes moved from Sim-Sung to me. "Do you have any money?" she asked.

I had been struck by her melodious voice. How well she spoke Korean! But I politely addressed her question.

"Oh, yes. My mother gave me three *won*, and I spent a little over one *won* to get here. So I have nearly two *won*," I answered confidently.

But instead of accepting my money, Miss Frey turned to Sim-Sung. "Do you intend to help her with room and board?"

Sim-Sung glanced quickly at me, as if apologizing. Then she answered respectfully, "No, I would not be able to do that."

"Then why did you bring her here without my consent?" Miss Frey leaned back in her chair. She seemed tired.

Sim-Sung looked uncomfortable and remained silent.

The blue-eyed woman turned back to me. "Is there someone who will pay for you?"

I shook my head.

"A child your age should have better sense than to think you can get an education on two *won*!"

"I thought this school was free," I ventured.

"Tuition is free, but room and board are not," explained Miss Frey.

She sighed and went on, "I do not know who has sent you. You have no sponsor. Therefore you will have to return home."

I drew in a breath to begin speaking, but Miss Frey's

voice had been firm. I remained silent.

"The day after tomorrow, one of our teachers is traveling to Pyongyang. You will accompany her. Good day, girls."

With that, the principal went back to the papers on her desk. I looked desperately at Sim-Sung, who only motioned to leave.

We walked through the hallways, now filled with students. Sim-Sung headed to the door, not saying a word until we reached the veranda.

"Induk, I'm so sorry! I have gotten you into a terrible situation."

I barely heard her. I was still trying to understand what had happened.

"You will have to go home, Induk," Sim-Sung said.

"But I can't!" I wailed in disbelief. "This is the only place where I can go to school!"

Sim-Sung shrugged. Her face was sad. "But Miss Frey will send you back."

"No," I declared. "I must convince her to let me stay. It's my only chance!"

"I am truly sorry, Induk," Sim-Sung went on, ignoring my determination. There was a pleading tone to her voice. "I thought that if your mother could not pay for your room and board they would find someone who could. I would never have suggested you come if I had thought this might happen!"

I heard Sim-Sung's words, but they did not matter

to me. I was desperately trying to think of a way that I could stay at Ewha.

Sim-Sung looked at me. "Induk, you will have to go home."

I shrugged. "We'll see. You'd better get to class. No use in you missing just because I can't go."

I spent the day wandering about the campus, feeling the enthusiasm of the other students. It made me all the more determined to stay. I began rehearsing in my mind what I would say to Miss Frey tomorrow. After all, I would not be put on the train until the following day.

The next morning, Sim-Sung left for class and I headed for the principal's office. As I sat on the bench again, I knew the tension of yesterday had been nothing compared to how I felt now.

Again I was ushered into the office. Miss Frey looked surprised to see me.

"Good morning, Induk. Your train does not leave until tomorrow."

"Good morning, Miss Frey. I wish to speak to you about my staying here and working for my room and board." I spoke politely but as firmly as my nervousness allowed.

Miss Frey frowned. "Room and board is three *won* a month. You say you have two *won*. That is not even enough for the first month."

"I can work! I can work for three *won*! I know I can!"

I said, trying to be respectful, but fearful that my chance to go to high school was quickly slipping away.

Miss Frey looked skeptical.

I could contain myself no longer. I burst out, "I must stay! Please let me stay! I can study hard and I will take care of myself! I did at Samsung."

This time Miss Frey's voice was low and very controlled. "Induk, your train leaves tomorrow. Be in my office at nine o'clock sharp to meet the teacher who will accompany you. Good day."

I longed to say more, but Miss Frey's manner was so final I knew it was hopeless. Quietly I walked out of the office, knowing that I had only one more chance.

I awoke the next morning after a restless sleep. Taking all my belongings from Sim-Sung's room, I headed toward the main building once again. I hoped desperately that I need not have packed, but to appear in the principal's office unprepared to leave would anger Miss Frey further.

"Good morning, Induk," Miss Frey said when I appeared in her doorway. "Your escort will be here shortly. I am glad you are punctual."

I took a deep breath.

"Miss Frey, my mother wants me to get an education more than anything else in the world. When my father and brother died, she disguised me as a boy so I could attend the boys' school in our village. For a year I attended school there and learned to read and write in

Chinese. The next year we moved so I could attend Samsung and be a girl again. Even though I was only eight years old, I lived at the school and cooked my own food because my mother had to work as a peddler to support me. She is still a peddler and will send as much money as she can. If you write to my teachers at Samsung, I know they will tell you that I was a very good student and that I studied hard. I'm sorry I came here without a sponsor, but I have no one who can sponsor me. This is the only place where I can get a high school education."

I stopped. My heart was pounding, I was out of breath. Could all of that really have come out of me?

Miss Frey remained silent. Her blue eyes studied me.

Afraid to say anything more, I stood, uncomfortable under the gaze of this powerful woman.

There was a noise behind me. I turned as Miss Frey glanced toward the door. There stood the teacher who was to accompany me to Pyongyang.

"Oh, Dr. Hall. Thank you for stopping. There's been a change of plans. Meet Induk Pahk, Ewha's newest student."

There was a gasping sound, and I realized it came from me.

"Good morning, Dr. Hall," I stammered, and turned back to Miss Frey to try to thank her.

But Miss Frey said quickly, "Well, run along, Induk. If you hurry you will be on time for your first class."

"Thank you! Oh, thank you!" I gushed, and with a grateful smile, I rushed to the door.

Miss Frey said only, "Hurry now!"

But she was smiling too.

CHAPTER FIVE

Learning Every Day

I sat down on the floor at a long, low table, my new rice bowl, spoon, and chopsticks in front of me. Sim-Sung sat next to me. We were in the dining room of Ewha High School, where each table seated eight girls, with an upperclass student at the head.

A teacher raised her hand for silence and said a meal blessing. As she finished, I became aware of a wonderful aroma in the room. Large trays of steaming food had been brought in. One was set before me since it was my turn to serve.

Never before had I seen so much food! Here were

bowls of rice with red beans, Korean pickled cabbage called *kimchi,* other vegetable dishes, and fish. Meat would be served tomorrow because it would be Friday.

It had been a busy, exciting week. As I served the other girls, I ventured to speak with them.

"I am having trouble with some of the English sounds," I admitted shyly.

"Let me guess," one of the older girls said with a twinkle in her eye. "Could it be 'f' or 'th'?" She pronounced them perfectly.

"Yes," I said, "And also 'z' and 'v'." I was embarrassed to say them, knowing I was mispronouncing them.

The other girl laughed, but not unkindly. "Oh, I know! I worked on them for months! Keep practicing them, Induk. You'll get them eventually. If I can, anyone can!"

"I do practice—" I started to say.

Sim-Sung handed me her bowl. "Yes you do, Induk, and you sound like a mad bee, 'z-ing' all the time! You'll get the 'th' sound before I do. It's so hard!"

I laughed, first at myself as a mad bee, then at Sim-Sung's attempts to pronounce 'th'.

"If you think the sounds of words are difficult, wait until music class," another girl added. "I started today. We learn American folk songs and they are different from Korean folk songs. They are done in harmony."

Interested, and too impatient to wait until my first

music class, I asked, "What is harmony?"

"One person sings the melody and another sings a little higher or lower. It is more difficult than singing the melody only, but it is pretty."

The next day was Friday, and I had gym class as well as music, math, and science. We stood in the large gymnasium, and I marveled at the size of the room. The instructor was talking about a game called basketball. She divided us into teams and we were to play together against the other team.

I puzzled over this. My culture always encouraged me to be in groups, but I had never known of this idea of working as a team.

"And of course," the American teacher said casually, "One team must lose. That is the way it is with games. One team wins, one loses."

One girl gasped, and we all began whispering together. We each had been taught that we must not lose.

The teacher seemed to expect this. She smiled and said, "Yes, one team will lose. You will win sometimes and lose sometimes. When you lose, it is not a disgrace."

Not a disgrace to lose! I was shocked. I would have to think about that one. I glanced at the faces of my classmates. They were as amazed as I was.

But soon I was in singing class, struggling with another new idea called singing in harmony. The instructor listened to me sing alone.

"You have a good voice, Induk. It is a bit low, so

you will sing alto."

Alto? Something else to wonder about! I worked in class to understand my part and spent all my spare time singing it, or practicing the 'th' and 'z' sounds.

That night, I moved my quilt and books into the room across from Sim-Sung. This new room assignment made me feel officially a part of Ewha, but I was glad Sim-Sung was nearby. Exhausted after a demanding week, I curled into my blue quilt and slept.

Saturday morning brought a new set of activities. I awoke to sounds in the hallway. Since there were no classes, I was puzzled by all the activity. Was I missing something?

Peeking out of my room, I saw several girls carrying pails and cleaning cloths, going down the stairs. Across the hall, Sim-Sung opened her door. She too had a pail in hand.

"Good morning, Induk," she called cheerily. "Cleaning day!"

Of course.

"Next week you and I are on general cleaning," Sim-Sung explained. "I checked the schedule last night. Several of us will have to clean the classroom, the chapel, halls, and stairways."

Laughter came from the stairs as this week's group did their chores.

"But this week, we just clean our rooms?" I asked, indicating Sim-Sung's pail.

"Yes, and ourselves! Bath and hair wash today," Sim-Sung explained, and then with less enthusiasm added, "And washing our clothes. Have you ever washed blouses?"

I had to confess that I hadn't. It was too difficult a task for a child to do by herself. Most girls learned under the watchful eyes of their mothers, but since I had not lived with my mother since I was eight years old, there had not been an opportunity for her to teach me. She had always given me a clean blouse when she visited me and taken the soiled one with her to wash.

"Then you're in for a treat," Sim-Sung said with a teasing grin.

A few hours later, I found out what Sim-Sung meant. Sitting with classmates in a large room, we each had our winter blouse in hand, taking it apart. Each blouse was made with ten pieces of cotton or silk for the outer part and seven pieces for the lining. Having taken each one apart, we washed all the soiled parts, starched all the parts, and allowed them to dry.

As I waited for mine to dry, I watched another girl fold her now dry pieces and lay them on a polished granite slab. She picked up a pair of smooth, round sticks and began beating the cloth in a rhythmic way. After a while the cloth began to shine with an unusual luster. Now she was finished with that part.

"Now you have to sew all the pieces back together?"

I asked.

She nodded wearily. "And then iron them with the charcoal iron."

It was not a fun task, and though it helped to be laughing and talking with others, the work seemed to go on and on.

"Hello, girls!" the music teacher called from the doorway. "Tedious job you have there. I have a suggestion. You can skip the beating part. Use this!"

She produced a flat iron from behind her back. "This will save you that step at least. Feel free to use it."

As she left, we looked at one another gratefully. Now we could get to our baths a little faster.

But Sunday was different. It was a quiet, restful day. In the morning, there was a Sunday school session, followed by a church service. Afterward, each of us was given a bun filled with sweetened bean pulp to be eaten alone in her room. After this simple meal, we were free to rest, read, write letters, or chat quietly.

I chose to write to my mother, delighted that we could both read and write now.

I told her about harmony, losing at basketball, about the new iron, and dinner conversations.

Ending the letter, I wrote, "The week here is very full, and I love this Sunday quiet. But I will welcome the activity beginning on Monday. I am learning so much and am so grateful for this opportunity for high school. I am studying hard and being brave! Your girl-son, Induk."

———— ❋ ————

One day in late autumn, I stacked my books into a pile.

"I won't need these for a whole week!" I thought, looking at each one as I piled them.

Mathematics, English, health, Chinese classics. My head still whirled at the thought of such subjects, but I was doing it! I, Induk, the girl-son, was learning these difficult things. Eventually, I vowed, I would join the debate class.

But not now. Now was pickling vacation, a good chance to relax and help the school too.

There was a knock at the door and Sim-Sung's voice called, "Ready, Induk?"

"Ready!"

We set off for the school kitchen where other students and teachers were already at work.

A food unique to Korea is *kimchi*. We have it at every meal, so a school like Ewha needs a large supply for the winter. Now that the harvest was in, it was time to start pickling.

Kimchi is not like sour dill pickles made with cucumbers. It is very spicy, filled with fiery red peppers, and many other vegetables. Cabbages, onions, garlic, carrots, turnips, celery, gingerroot, and even chestnuts joined the pile of brilliant red peppers on the tables.

Girls and teachers were laughing and talking as they worked, the aroma of onions and garlic filling the room.

After shredding a head of cabbage, I took my bowl to Miss Frey. First she washed and drained the vegetable, then sprinkled teaspoons of salt over it. I watched, thinking of all the times I had seen Mother do this. The cabbage would become limp soon, and then various combinations of the other vegetables and some salted fish would be added. The mixture would then be allowed to rest, or pickle.

"The batch over here is ready, Induk. Do you want to come with me to store it?" Miss Frey invited.

We carried the heavy earthen jars filled with the new *kimchi* to a storeroom that had been dug out of the earth. Carefully, we descended the dark stairs, unsteady under the weight of the cumbersome jars. The storeroom was cold, colder than the autumn day above. We placed the jars on a shelf where other jars already waited.

In the corner was a large pile of husks, torn from harvested rice plants.

"Bring a bundle of husks here, Induk," Miss Frey directed. "We will cover all these jars with them."

Scooping up an armful of husks, I followed Miss Frey's example of padding the jars with them.

"Why are we doing this?" I asked. "My mother does this too, but I never asked why."

"Always ask why, Induk," Miss Frey said, smiling at me. "Did you notice that it is colder in here than above ground?"

I nodded.

"It will get very cold down here this winter and we don't want the *kimchi* to freeze. The rice husks are insulation. They will keep it from getting cold enough to freeze."

"Insulation," I repeated.

A new word. A new idea.

————— ❀ —————

The days after pickling vacation sped by. Winter set in, and with it, Christmas preparations began. Each Christmas Eve, Miss Frey invited the girls to her apartment, in small groups. Excitedly, I walked through the snow with a few other girls to Miss Frey's home.

"Do you remember the tree she had last year?" one girl said.

"Yes, full of candles and angels!" another answered dreamily.

I remained silent, but with each step my excitement grew.

We reached the apartment. Miss Frey greeted each of us with a friendly smile, wishing us a merry Christmas.

And then I saw it. The tree was standing in the corner. Its branches were filled with treasures: colored balls that shimmered in the light, small candles that gave a soft glow to the room, pictures of winged angels singing, playing harps, and proclaiming the good news, and little shepherds lovingly tending their sheep. Wisps of white cotton rested lightly on the branches too, making it look as if snow had just fallen. I gazed, enchanted.

Miss Frey broke my reverie. "Girls, have a seat, please. There are gifts for each of you."

At the foot of that lovely tree was a stack of boxes, each wrapped in shiny paper with designs on it, and tied with gaily colored ribbon. The principal handed each of us a gift and explained, "These gifts are from people who attend Methodist churches in the United States. They wish you a merry Christmas."

The girls whispered excitedly, but now and then a squeal of delight filled the room as a student opened her gift. But I sat by the beautiful tree and lovingly touched the bright paper and soft red ribbon on mine. I didn't want to tear the paper. I didn't want to give up this moment. I was sure that having a gift and not knowing what was in it was better than after it was opened.

"Open yours, Induk!" Sim-Sung urged.

I slid my finger under the wrap, careful not to tear the paper. There were several gifts inside the box! First, I opened a small box and discovered a bar of soap. It was smooth, except where an English word had been carved into it in a lovely script. I liked the hard, waxy texture, so I caressed my cheek with it. Then I discovered that the soap had a pleasant fragrance. I hoped I, too, would have this scent after I washed with it. Also, there was a washcloth—a bright yellow, nubby cloth all my own.

Tucked in among these was a Christmas card. It showed a serene little village, covered in snow. But the cottages were not thatched like ours. These must be American houses. I studied them intently. On the back were the English words, "Merry Christmas!"

Best of all, under these gifts, was a long, flannel nightgown. It was soft as a kitten and would be wonderfully warm on these frigid winter nights. I held it up. It was white, with stripes of blue flowers. It was the first real nightgown I had ever owned.

Sim-Sung smiled at me.

"I wish I could thank the people who sent this!" I whispered to her.

"One more thing, girls," Miss Frey announced, and she gave each of us a bag.

Peeking inside, I saw a tangerine, peanuts, and taffy, gifts from the school. Never before had I gotten so many presents!

After everyone had admired each other's new treasures, we began to sing Christmas carols. As I sang—alto—I thought back to the time, long ago now, when I had first heard these songs. It was the day I had received my pencil in the church near my first home. How my life had changed since then! As I stroked my new nightgown, I realized my greatest gift was my mother's strong belief that I should go to school.

When we could sing no more, we played games. Finally, it was time to leave. Trudging across the campus to our rooms, the December wind was chilling, but I was warm with the laughter of the evening and the friendships I had made this year.

"Sleep well," Sim-Sung wished me as we headed to our rooms.

Pointing to my nightgown, I answered, "Of course!"

———— ✸ ————

As the school year progressed, I added other activities to my workload: public speaking classes, training to conduct meetings, and the debate team.

"Next week's topic for discussion will be the necessity for women to receive higher education, pro and con," the teacher announced at a meeting of the debate team. "Here's something to think about as you prepare—for generations, girls have been taught that women must be silent and meek. Think of the changes education will bring. I look forward to your presentations."

Slowly I walked back to my room. Images of my mother came to me. Her name, Onyu, means "meek." My grandparents had given her that name to assure that she be just that. It didn't work, I thought with a chuckle. My father had given me the name Imduk, meaning virtuous woman. To him, that had meant meek too. But Mother had renamed me Induk, one who does kindnesses.

Perhaps that was one of the good things of education—that one would be freed and could do kindnesses, like Miss Frey and the teachers. With their educations, they were helping my classmates and me.

Possibly someday, I would do good things for Korea because I had been given the opportunity for an education.

I began running back to my room so I could write down that thought before I could lose it.

———— ◉ ————

Spring had arrived in Seoul. The campus was pink and white with flowers, the air rich with the scent. I especially loved the cherry blossoms.

I shifted my books from one arm to the other. So much had happened this year! But now I was worried. When Mother had learned that I had been wrong in assuming there were no school expenses, and Miss Frey had accepted me without a sponsor, Mother promised to pay one-third of the money. She did so hoping I would not need to work but could instead devote myself to study. Also, Mr. John Z. Moore, an American family friend living in Pyongyang, heard of my situation and offered to pay the other two-thirds. Would Mother earn that much money for next year? Could Mr. Moore continue to contribute? I did not want to leave Ewha, but I knew that staying here was far from certain.

A few days later, I was summoned to Miss Frey's office. I raced down the hallway. Was something wrong? Had something happened to Mother?

When I entered the office I knew immediately that nothing was wrong. Miss Frey's blue eyes sparkled with excitement.

"Induk, I was able to secure a scholarship for you. There is a man in Wilmington, Illinois—that is in the United States—named C. G. Steinhart. He and his sister and brother-in-law have sent thirty-five dollars to cover your first year's expenses."

My mouth fell open in amazement. Thirty-five dollars!

"Mr. Steinhart is blind. He became blind at the age of nineteen. He has sent a picture of himself."

Hands shaking, I took the picture. In it sat a smiling, Caucasian man. Suddenly I was blinking back tears.

"There's more," Miss Frey said. "They have promised the same amount for the next two years of high school—"

I interrupted her with a little cry of delight, but she held up her hand and continued.

"And for four years of college."

This time I lost my voice. I only looked wonderingly at the principal.

Miss Frey chuckled with pleasure. "Yes, Induk, it's true! You can finish high school and go to college! I've written to your mother. I will refund all the money she has paid for this year."

I sat down, though Miss Frey had not directed me to do so.

"I hardly know what to say," I said slowly. I looked again at the picture in my hand. "These people do not even know me!"

Smiling, Miss Frey handed me a letter. "This is from Mr. Steinhart."

The letter was on white paper, single-spaced, and three pages long. It was in English.

"He wants you to know that you have brought a new interest into his life, Induk. He very much hopes to meet you one day. He also says he hopes you'll study hard because the whole world lies ahead of you."

I assured Miss Frey that I would study hard, thanked her, and left.

Outside, I paused to soak in the spring sunshine. The delicate buds on the trees were a pale, young green. Small flowers peeked up along the walkways. Everything spoke of newness and promise.

Hugging the letter to my heart, I whispered, "The whole world lies ahead of me!"

CHAPTER SIX

From Teacher
to Prisoner

While I studied in my high school classes, Miss Frey was working to start Ewha College. Any education for girls, but especially college, was opposed by many people in Korea then, and Miss Frey met conflicts and criticism every step of the way. But in 1909, with little fanfare, Ewha College opened. It was housed in the high school building and boasted three students.

Two years later, now a high school graduate, I began college classes with two other young women. Before graduation, however, the other two had left and I was often alone in my classes.

One evening, I sat at my desk, surrounded by books. Tomorrow, I had English, mathematics, and history. Miss Alice R. Appenzeller was both my English and my history instructor. To go to classes unprepared was unthinkable, when I had her for two classes and I was the only student in each!

Tonight I struggled over my history book. The only text available to me for college level was written in English, so I had the extra task of translating the reading assignment before I could learn it.

There was a soft knock at my door. It was Chang-Soon, one of the younger students in the class behind mine. "I'm taking a little break. Mind if I come in?"

"No," I answered gratefully. "I'd like a break myself. I feel as if my mind could pop like a balloon, I've put so much into it!"

Chang-Soon nodded. "Yes, sometimes I want to give up. I look at girls I knew when I was a child—even girls we knew here in high school. They are getting married and having babies. They don't bend over books and study till all hours of the night."

"Yes, but they are bending over hot stoves. They are up with babies at night. We may marry and have children eventually, but we are so lucky, Chang-Soon! Do you think there have been any other women in the history of Korea who have learned what we are studying? We are part of the world, not just part of a household!"

Chang-Soon smiled. "Yes, you are right, Induk. I guess I'm just tired tonight. And a little worried. Being part of the world, as you say, gives me plenty to worry about."

I had to agree, and did so with a deep sigh. The year before, the country of Japan had annexed Korea. By forcefully taking over, the Japanese now controlled my country. Life had not been the same since. Japanese flags had gone up everywhere. The Japanese language was now taught in all schools. Koreans no longer had freedom of speech, of the press, or of religion.

It was under these conditions that I finished my college degree. There could be little celebration, but Mother wrote to say how proud she was of her girl-son. She had always known I could do it. I read the letter with misted eyes and wondered what I could do with my education.

But I did not have to wonder long. Miss Frey asked me to stay on—as a teacher for both the high school and college. I was deeply honored and very pleased to give back a fraction of what she had given me. Despite the fact that college for women was frowned upon by the Japanese, I entered the teaching profession eagerly. Within days of graduation, I was back in the classroom, teaching math, physical education, and music. Now I had to teach singing in harmony!

By 1919, the Western world was ending a great world

war. The Japanese government had ruled Korea for nine years. The Koreans were angry, fighting angry. Our beloved King Kojong had been forced to leave his throne some years earlier. When he died of unknown causes, it was rumored that he had been killed. That rumor was like a match to dry firewood.

March 1, 1919, was the day of public mourning for the king. In Pagoda Park, in Seoul, thirty-three well-known Korean men gathered and signed a Declaration of Independence. One read it aloud and soon a large crowd gathered, shouting for freedom.

From that day on, there were more demonstrations in Seoul, and also in villages and towns. The Japanese police arrested many of the demonstrators, and the jails were overflowing with ordinary people who wanted Korea to be free.

Soon I, too, would be one of these people.

During some of the demonstrations in Seoul, I joined the crowds. Surrounded by waving flags and my fellow Koreans, I felt great love for my country, and a deep desire for freedom. I, too, cheered, calling for liberty.

Ten days after the protest in Pagoda Park, I was teaching a class on geometry. There was a knock at the door and a student messenger said quietly, "Miss Pahk, Miss Frey would like to see you in her office immediately."

Quickly I instructed a student to take over. Miss Frey rarely called her teachers away from their classes.

Hurrying to the office, I felt my heart pounding wildly. What was wrong?

The open door revealed two police officers in Miss Frey's office. I saw fear in her eyes, though she sat tall and commanding at her desk.

Before either she or I could speak, one of the officers said gruffly, "Induk Pahk, you have been participating in the demonstrations against the Japanese government. We are here to arrest you."

Immediately, he produced a rope. I stared at it in horror.

Miss Frey rose and stepped toward me. In a strong voice she said, "You need not tie her. She will not try to run away."

"It is a regulation," he said curtly.

He slipped the rope around my waist and tied it. I felt like an animal. He and the other officer took the other end of the rope and began leading me out of Miss Frey's office.

"I'm going with her," Miss Frey said firmly and followed.

Terror was filling me like water poured into a jug. I wanted to thank Miss Frey for coming with me, but I sensed silence was expected of me. I was a prisoner.

We walked to the police station. At the gate, one officer turned to Miss Frey.

"This is as far as you may go."

"You cannot just take her away from me, from the school! She is in my employ!" Miss Frey protested, her voice angry and full of fear.

The officers did not respond with words. Instead, one grabbed her and held her back, as the other clutched that horrid rope tighter and led me through the looming iron gate.

Convinced she was powerless to help me herself now, she said to me in English, "Trust in God!"

———— ✲ ————

Inside the police station, I was led to a row of cages, and thrust into one. A woman guard entered with me, taking my hair pins and ribbon.

"We don't want you trying to hurt yourself with these," the woman said bluntly. "Now follow me."

She led me to an examination room. Though it was dimly lit, I could see sticks, ropes, and hoses. I had been scared before, but I had never known terror as I did then. I knew these objects were used for torturing people.

Four men stood there, their gazes heavily on me. One, the examiner, spoke. "Sit down."

It was not an invitation. He motioned to a bench against the wall. Quickly, I sat.

"You are a teacher," he said. "Therefore you are responsible for all your students who have joined the demonstrations for independence. For this you should be punished. What do you have to say about this?"

"I cannot prevent my students from taking part in what is right. I am not responsible for their conduct." Despite my brave words, my voice betrayed my fear.

Immediately a guard was standing over me. He was a burly man, and he held a large bamboo stick. His arm was raised above my head.

Instinctively, I braced myself for the blow, but Miss Frey's words came back to me. I prayed silently. With no explanation, the guard dropped his hand. The examiner motioned for the guard to lead me back to the cage. Not a word was spoken.

The sound of the door clanging shut behind me did not even bother me. I sank to the floor, shaking. I knew that it was common for others to leave the examination room bruised and bleeding.

Hours passed, but no one came for me. I was relieved and resigned myself to spending the night sitting on the floor of this cage. I dozed, but woke frequently at sounds from other parts of the building.

Morning came. I opened my eyes to see a woman being led from the examining room. Blood was coming from her mouth.

"When will it be my turn?" I wondered silently, and hoped that I could be strong.

Noon came and went. The hours dragged by, but they were more easily endured than being beaten. Each time a guard was within sight, I hoped he wasn't coming in my direction.

Finally, it was evening. The smallness of the cage was stifling, but I did not dare to complain. As night came on, again I sank wearily to the floor, accepting another restless sleep.

Around midnight, the sound of keys in the door of the cage startled me awake. Groggy but instantly frightened, I saw a guard standing in the doorway. He handed me a bag containing my possessions, the hair ribbons and pins taken from me earlier.

"Follow me," he said.

On shaking legs, I followed the man out of the station to a waiting car.

"Get in."

Slowly, I began to feel something beyond fear. Though I dared not speak, my mind began racing with excitement.

"That was it! I am going back to Ewha!" I thought as I looked hungrily out the car window at the familiar streets.

But the car did not slow down when it reached Ewha.

"Oh, no!" I thought desperately. "Where are they taking me?"

My high hopes fell like a rock into a lake. I felt more fear than when I had been led away from Ewha.

Moments later, I knew my destination: West Gate Prison. The heavy gate swung open and the car passed through. The driver stopped and said simply, "Get out."

Clutching my possessions, I stumbled out of the car. Two female guards were waiting to take me through another gate and into a looming building. Down a hallway we marched. After we entered a room, the two guards began undressing me, searching for weapons. When they were satisfied that I was not dangerous, they handed me a prison uniform. Hastily I pulled it on, and one guard pinned a strip of cloth on it. It said, "Number 2221." Again I was led to an unknown destination.

It was one o'clock in the morning. I had experienced fear for two days now. I had had very little sleep or food. Yet I felt completely alert, not knowing what lay ahead.

Soon I was led to a hallway with numbered doors. This was solitary confinement. I was to be imprisoned alone and would not be permitted to talk with anyone.

The guards stopped me at a cell marked number six. The thick wooden door was pushed open. I had no choice but to enter. A guard pulled the door shut with a bang. The sound of a heavy bolt being drawn was all that met my ears. I felt as if I were being sealed in a tomb.

I looked around. The cell was about six feet by six feet, and nine feet tall. There was one window near the ceiling, too high for me to see out. Two rows of bars and heavy screen covered it.

In one corner hung a light bulb. It gave off barely enough brightness to see the other aspects of the room. Another corner held a box to be used as a toilet. A putrid smell rose from it.

Then I saw a bucket with a dipper. A small hope rose in me. I looked in, hoping for a drink of water. It was empty.

There was no bed, just a lump of blanket on the floor. In the feeble light I examined it. It was filthy and infested with bugs.

What could I do but sit on the floor? I heard guards pass quietly back and forth. At one point, I heard more footsteps and the bang of a nearby door. Another prisoner had been brought into the cell next to mine.

With nothing else to look at, I began examining the door. It had three openings: one was a peephole, placed at eye level from the floor, and about the size of an eye; another was in the middle and about a foot square; the third was a shuttered ventilator near the bottom.

At what I guessed to be about five-thirty in the morning, loud voices yelled, "Get up! Get up!"

Not knowing what to expect, I stood up, trying to feel a little less vulnerable.

The peephole opened and an eye peered in.

"You!" a gruff voice barked, "Sit down on your knees and face the door. Stay that way. Break this rule and you'll be beaten."

The peephole door slammed shut. I got onto my knees, listening to other prisoners being told to do the same thing.

Soon a cup of water was thrust through the square opening. Gratefully, I drank it. There was more noise in the hallway, and I could vaguely smell food. In vain I tried not to think of the nourishing food at Ewha as I waited for this food, my knees already beginning to ache.

The square door opened again. I could see part of the clay-colored uniform of another prisoner who delivered breakfast. Anxiously I searched the tray that was pushed into the cell. A handful of boiled soybeans, millet, and a tiny bit of sandy rice lay there. Next to it was a small bowl containing a salty, watery soup with bits of vegetables floating in it. Hungrily I ate, not daring to move off of my knees.

It was a long morning, having started before dawn. The cold March wind howled in the window above. I thought of the classes I would be teaching today if I were free.

Free. I hadn't really grappled with that word since the arrest.

And I could not now. My knees ached. My eyes ached. I had not really slept in a long, long time.

Finally there was a noise in the hallway. Lunch was being served. Again, a small bit of hope rose in me.

"At least it is something to do," I told myself. "And I am so hungry!"

The food thrust into my cell was the same as breakfast, only salt had been added. Disappointed, I ate, knowing I must keep my strength up as best I could.

At five-thirty, guards came around and began opening cell doors. Two checked on me quickly. I could hear other prisoners now. Some were moaning, others crying.

Most were just ordinary people, taken from their families, homes, work, friends. Even though I had never met any of these other prisoners, I longed to call out, "I understand! I am crying myself!"

But of course, I remained silent, sitting on my legs.

Dinner arrived, the same food as breakfast and lunch, with a small amount of salted fish added. I longed for water, but no more came.

Mercifully, nine-thirty arrived, when we were allowed to sleep. I eased off of my sore legs, lay down on the unyielding, cold floor, and vowed, "If I survive this, I will never, never cause anyone to suffer!"

CHAPTER SEVEN

Many Kinds of Freedom

I soon learned the prison routine. Every other day the toilet boxes were removed and emptied, but never cleaned. Once a week, a woman guard took me to a bathing room. The water was filmy and dark.

"I wonder how many other prisoners have used this water before me?" I thought. One look at the guard told me not to ask. Instead I concentrated on enjoying being let out of my cell.

As I was being led back to my cell, I wondered about this woman who guarded me. She had her freedom, and I did not, but was she truly free? Because of the invasion of one country by another, she must work here, causing others great distress. As she slammed the cell door, I looked at her unreadable face. Maybe she had a daughter somewhere. Maybe she had been a child who had loved to listen to her grandmother's stories. Yet, today she was locking me into a prison. Was she free?

A few days after my imprisonment, I learned that inmates did not have to wear prison clothing if someone was willing to supply them with their own. A friend from Ewha sent me clean clothing on a regular basis, and, best of all, a clean quilt and pillow. I hugged that pillow. Ah, to sleep again!

The first days passed into weeks. Waking at five-thirty and sitting on my knees until nine-thirty at night was as difficult as waiting in fear. My legs became swollen. One day I realized, to my horror, that they were turning black. I worried that if this imprisonment lasted much longer, I might lose the use of my legs.

And then there was time. As a child, I was unaware of time. As a student, I saw time as a way to mark different classes. As I grew older, I used time for studying and wondered if I had enough. Now, time was my enemy. It passed at a snail's pace.

I told myself that each day drew me closer to my release, but still they passed by agonizingly slowly. I dared not think about any other possibility but release.

To cope, I began to recall events from my past. I would think of people and try to remember every detail of their faces and clothes. First, the wrinkled face of my kindly teacher, back in Monyangtul. Sim-Sung's laughing face came back quickly, and I wondered where she was now. Of course, I thought of Mother, wondering if Miss Frey had contacted her about my arrest. I even recalled moments with my father, who had loved me despite his disappointment at my birth. I imagined being able to talk with him now. How impressed he would be to see his daughter teaching college!

And then bang! Some noise from the hallway would break my concentration. All over again, I had to accept that I was not a college teacher now, I was a prisoner. And the slow passage of hours seemed deadly.

My only hope was to be called to court. Perhaps then I would be freed.

Being constantly alone began to wear on me. Days of friendship and class work at Ewha seemed a long time ago. Never far from hunger, I diligently ate the monotonous food, but it was never enough. All along I had been praying, but now I began praying for two things: food and a Bible.

March turned to April, I guessed. Now it was close to May. One day the small door opened and a tray of food was pushed in. It was time for the regular noon meal, but the aroma that rose from those dishes alerted me. Something was different!

However, before I could inspect the tray, something else was thrust into the cell. I gasped. It was a Bible! Clutching the book, I laughed and cried at the same time.

Then I looked at the tray. Instead of the meager prison food, this held well-cooked rice with broiled beef, bean sprouts, and *kimchi*. Eagerly I ate and began to read.

Not till later did I learn that these precious gifts came to me through Miss Frey and other American friends. Because of their foreign status in Korea, they were able to do more for me than my Korean friends could.

Anxiously I waited that evening to see if the good food was to continue, for I had no idea why it had come. Much to my relief, from then on, twice a day, nourishing food was brought to me. The rest of the day I spent poring over the Bible. I studied the maps in the back of the book, and I read between eight to fourteen hours a day.

Though I read extensively, I was drawn to St. Paul the most because he had been imprisoned for his work in the early Christian Church. With no one to talk to, and hours of reading each day, I began having a strong feeling that Paul's life was to be an example for me. I had been given a tremendous amount in my life. Now I had much to give. What work could I do after I got out of prison? Certainly all the unusual events of my life were to lead to some good!

These thoughts helped carry me through the days. It was now early summer. I had been sitting on my legs in this cell for almost three months. Though the time still dragged on with little hope of a court hearing, I was better able to cope as I was no longer hungry and my mind was occupied.

Because of my improved nutrition and better state of mind, I had begun to look better. One day a woman guard came and led me to an office. There a Canadian missionary was waiting for me.

"See?" said a police officer in the room. "She is well provided for!"

Several other times I was fetched from my cell for foreign visitors to look me over. They went away with a good impression of the prison, which angered me because good treatment was the work of my friends, not the prison officials. However, there was nothing I could say with guards and prison officials present. Of course, the guards were pleased with the impression I gave and after that I was taken outside for fifteen minutes every day. I was never told why, but each time the guard arrived to take me out, she put a large hat on my head that covered my face. As I walked around the courtyard, the guard was never more than a step behind me. Still, the fresh air and sunshine on my shoulders was a precious gift. The exercise, short though it was, helped my sore legs too. Their color returned to normal and some strength returned.

Then one day the cell door swung open, although I had already had my brief outside time. Startled, I looked up from my Bible. A little gasp escaped from me, for there stood Miss Frey. A male guard stood with her.

"You must not speak, either of you," the guard said quickly.

I studied Miss Frey, hungry for the companionship of my friend and old life. Her eyes spoke of love and support. Neither of us attempted to speak, knowing that provoking the guard would have ended our time together. But we both understood how much we cared for each other and that we would both change all of this if we had the power.

Then just as suddenly, the guard banged the door shut.

I sat there, staring at the back of the closed door, feeling its solid presence with more hate than ever before. I ached to be able to pull open the door and run after Miss Frey, who was no doubt being led back to the street by the guard. Then rage filled me, and I began to sob.

A few days later, as I was obediently sitting on my legs and reading, the cell door again swung open. This time there was only a guard, with a rope in his hand.

Fear shot through my body with the speed of lightning. I dared not speak.

The guard tied the rope around my waist and led me

to a cart waiting outside of the prison. I was being taken to court!

Hope gradually began replacing the fear. The air, though muggy with summer heat, seemed wonderfully fresh! I breathed in deeply, as I blinked in the sunlight. Had the daytime always been so bright? I enjoyed every inch of that mile-long journey, seeing the streets of Seoul again.

But on arriving at court, my spirits sank again, and that old companion, fear, returned. As I was led to a tiny prisoner's box to await my hearing, I saw a man who had been tortured.

My cage was only large enough to stand in. My legs, still not back to normal strength, throbbed as I stood. The day became hotter, and I was given neither food nor water.

When not coping with hunger and pain, I was plagued with nervousness. What might happen in the courtroom? After days of longing for a hearing, I found myself thinking that my dark, silent prison cell seemed comfortable compared to the fear and discomfort in this cage.

Hours passed. No one approached my box until late in the afternoon, when I was led into the courtroom.

The judge said, "I hear you are a model prisoner. You have behaved well. But you must remember that you cannot gain freedom by fighting for it. You need to be obedient, to be a good wife and mother. We do not want you to teach young Korean girls such wild ideas of independence. If you promise to do as we say, I will have you released."

I remained respectfully quiet, as I had seen other prisoners do. I was glad that silence was what was expected of me since it would have been hard to agree to what the judge had said.

Within the hour, I was back in my cell at West Gate Prison. Again I stared at the closed, barred door.

"Oh, so many feelings!" I thought. "After all the fear today, it almost feels safe to be in here. Yet it is so hateful! I long to be free, to walk those streets myself! To talk with friends, to teach my classes! What did the judge mean, that I'll be released? When? Can I go back to Ewha? How much longer must I sit here in this tomb?"

Days dragged by. Summer heat hung over the cell like a heavy blanket. The odor from the toilet was stronger than ever.

By day, I waited, read, and sat on sweating, aching legs. I cried myself to sleep.

Then the door swung open again. As before, I was tied and taken to court in a cart. I tried desperately not to get my hopes up, but as I stood before the same judge, my heart pounded with anticipation.

"You are to be released under fifteen dollars bond. Your American friends have posted that bond. You may go."

Elation poured through my whole body. I could have turned cartwheels and sang a song. Instead, I quietly followed yet another guard to a black carriage.

Inside the carriage were three other Ewha women, Esther Whang, Maria Kim, and Julia Syn. I greeted them joyfully. They, too, had just been released from prison.

"What a gift this is, just to talk with someone!" I said. "It has been three months since I have had a conversation with anyone!"

Once more, I was heading for West Gate Prison, but with none of the fear and anger. There, we four were given our possessions back.

I looked at the hair ribbon, taken so roughly from me that long-ago day of my arrest. When I had put it in that morning, I had no idea what lay ahead of me. I rubbed my thumb over its smoothness. I knew I would never be the same person as I was on that March day that began so innocently.

A guard gave us instructions on what we could and could not do when we left, for we were on parole. It would be a few months before I could travel to see Mother.

With my friends, I then approached that formidable iron gate. Beyond it was freedom!

I walked toward it, thinking about my participation at the demonstrations. I had thought I knew what freedom was then. I wanted my country to make its own laws, to speak its own language and make its own decisions. That was right and good.

But now I understood that there were many more kinds of freedom. My mother had freed me by refusing to comply with the traditions that limited me. Miss Frey and many teachers had given me freedom by training me to think in new ways. There was the freedom to do one's work, to care for one's body in a healthy way, to choose one's religion.

In the distance, I could see both Korean and American friends waiting for me. On either side of me, guards stood bayonets poised in their arms. I looked at each one.

"These men are not free," I thought. "There are many kinds of prisons, and just as many kinds of freedoms."

One guard opened the massive gate, just enough for one person to pass through. In turn, each us of slipped through.

It was July 24, 1919. I had been in West Gate Prison for one hundred and thirty-six days.

Our waiting friends rushed to us, and tears and words flowed freely. I had forgotten how wonderful was the feeling of a loved one's arms about me.

As we headed toward Ewha, I looked back to the prison. I was haunted by the idea of prisons and freedoms.

Turning, I faced the direction of Ewha and made a vow: I would use my freedom and education to free others from the many kinds of prisons. And I would do so in a loud and clear voice.

EPILOGUE

Induk Pahk spent her adult life giving others freedom through education. After prison, Induk was allowed to return to teaching. She met a young man and they were married. Her mother and friends were against Induk's decision, feeling the man would not be able to accept her unusual life and plans. A few years later, now the mother of two daughters, Induk had to face the fact that the others were correct. She and her husband parted and Induk was left to support her family.

At that time, she was offered the opportunity she had longed for all her childhood: to travel to the United States. There she could study at Wesleyan College in Georgia. If she did so, she would be better able to provide for her daughters later. However, she would have to leave them in Korea with their grandmother while she was gone. Tradition dictated that it must be the father's mother who would be responsible for the children. It was not unusual in Korea for grandmothers to care for children and Induk knew her daughters would be loved and watched over carefully. She left Korea with mixed feelings: deeply saddened at having to leave her children and very excited about her chance to travel and study. Perhaps it was then that she understood how hard it was for her mother when she had left eight-year-old Induk at school.

Induk knew when she first sailed on board a ship to the United States that she was fulfilling her childhood dream, but she didn't realize she was beginning a life of extensive travel.

Induk spent five years in the United States. After completing her education, she traveled one hundred thousand miles by bus, over the United States and Canada. On college campuses, she spoke of her then little-known country, encouraging students to work in poor countries.

On her way home, she fulfilled another dream of seeing many parts of the world. She traveled through England, Denmark, Germany, the Soviet Union, Greece, China, and other countries, studying farming and teaching methods. She was determined to bring home practical knowledge to help her people.

When she returned to Korea, she made a home for her mother and daughters. Both girls attended Ewha.

Induk worked to improve life for poor farm families. She taught children and mothers to read and write. When they had no pencils, they practiced writing in the dirt with sticks. Also, she wrote books to improve farming and educational systems.

All this led to Induk's greatest work: the founding of

a school.

While traveling, Induk spoke at Berea College in Kentucky, where students could learn job skills while earning money to pay for their education. Induk felt this was the best model for Korean farm children. She vowed that day to start "Berea in Korea."

She met with many difficulties and setbacks, but slowly she was able to purchase land, build a campus, hire teachers, and register students. On March 20, 1964, thirty-five years after Induk had made her vow, the Induk Vocational School for Boys officially opened. By the 1980s, Induk's "Berea in Korea" welcomed both boys and girls and had grown into two institutions: the Induk Technical High School, enrolling two thousand students, and the Induk Institute of Design, with over three thousand students.

She accomplished most of her work in a world occupied with war. World War II greatly affected her projects. Then her beloved Korea was divided and devastated by yet another war. She lost family and friends, and experienced hunger and poverty in those years.

Onyu, Induk's mother, was able to buy a house and support herself by weaving and peddling. When Induk built a home for herself and her daughters, Onyu agreed to live with them, only if she was needed. Together they lived simply but happily, with Onyu proud of Induk's work. Onyu died at the age of eighty-five.

Induk never saw Miss Frey after the brief prison visit. Miss Frey returned to the United States before Induk was released and she died before Induk traveled to the United States. Ewha High School and College is now Ewha Women's University, the largest university for women in the world.

To Induk's great pleasure, she met C. G. Steinhart, the blind man who had sponsored her at Ewha. He asked Induk to use her physical and spiritual sight to see the sick, lonely, and hungry people of the world.

She continued to learn, taking up swimming while in her twenties, skating in her thirties, the Japanese language in her forties, and driving in her fifties.

Induk died in 1980. She was eighty-four years old. Though Induk's father never knew her as a "girl-son," his prediction at her birth came true. She did indeed lead an extraordinary life.

BIRTH SIGNS

When Induk was born, her parents immediately checked her birth signs to predict her future. Induk herself felt her life reflected these signs.

Often called the Chinese zodiac, the signs are set in a cycle of twelve symbols with an animal representing each. The personalities of these animals are believed to influence certain times. One symbol is assigned to each year, month, day, and hour, so every person is born under four signs.

There are legends about how these animals were chosen and why the rat comes first. One story tells that when the founder of the Buddhist religion, called Buddha, was dying, many people and animals hurried to be with him. Of the animals, only twelve reached him. The clever rat got there first by riding on the large and powerful ox, then leaping off quickly to reach Buddha's bedside before anyone else. These twelve animals were given the honor of symbolizing the zodiac, and the rat sign is first.

CHARACTERISTICS OF EACH SIGN

THE SIGN OF THE RAT

Those born in the time of the rat are clever, energetic, ambitious, honest, and charming. Despite these traits, they are humble, even timid. They may be quick to anger, prone to gossip, and willing to spend freely on something they like but reluctant to do so for others. Rats are usually easy to get along with, are sentimental, and love to read.

The Rat gets along well with the Dragon and the Monkey. Avoid the Horse.

THE SIGN OF THE OX

(sometimes called the cow)

People born in the time of the Ox are intelligent, quiet, and powerful. These down-to-earth people are also patient, easygoing, hardworking, and rarely concerned about what others think. In a tense situation, it will be an Ox who will calm a group down and inspire confidence in others. However, they can be narrow-minded and stubborn.

The Ox gets along well with the Snake and the Rooster. Avoid the Sheep.

THE SIGN OF THE TIGER

Tigers are born with a fighting spirit. They are adventurous, wild, and courageous. Despite this, they are deep and sensitive thinkers. They have many friends, but are wary of strangers. Tigers like to be unconventional. Their tempers might give them trouble, and decisions are difficult for them.

The Tiger gets along well with the Horse and the Dog. Avoid the Monkey.

 ## THE SIGN OF THE RABBIT
(sometimes called the hare)

These people are caring and give and receive affection easily. They make others feel special by treating them with good manners. They are graceful and talented but are not showy. Rabbits can hang back in a group, not wanting to cause trouble. They can get depressed, and they are not often curious.

The Rabbit gets along well with the Sheep and the Boar. Avoid the Rooster.

THE SIGN OF THE DRAGON

Dragons are the most powerful of all the signs. They are natural leaders, honest, and talkative. Full of energy and good health, they often take risks and lead exciting lives. Very sensitive, they may be fretful, excitable, short-tempered, and stubborn. Their zest for life can make them critical of people who do not share their interests. Despite this, they are loved by others.

The Dragon gets along well with the Monkey and the Rat. Avoid the Dog.

 # THE SIGN OF THE SNAKE
(sometimes called the serpent)

Very intense and wise, the Snake has a deep and quiet personality. Often passionate, snakes can sometimes feel too much for others. Yet, they can be skeptical and self-centered. They are elegant and care about appearances. They have great determination and will make money.

The Snake gets along well with the Rooster and the Ox. Avoid the Boar.

THE SIGN OF THE HORSE

Those born in the time of the Horse have many friends. They are cheerful, energetic, and love to be outdoors. They are attractive and dress in a showy, colorful way. Horses know how to get their way, how to use money well, and are often winners at what they try. Horses can also be impulsive and stubborn.

The Horse gets along well with the Tiger and the Dog. Avoid the Rat.

THE SIGN OF THE SHEEP

Energetic and creative, sheep are elegant in what they do and how they look. Best at the arts, their talents will bring them money. They are gentle, but also timid and tend to worry. Sheep are very sensitive toward other people and their surroundings.

The Sheep gets along well with the Boar and the Rabbit. Avoid the Ox.

THE SIGN OF THE MONKEY

Since monkeys are high achievers and can influence and motivate others, they are good and clever politicians. They have a love for knowledge and are creative, talented, and self-willed. Although they are big thinkers and doers, they can become discouraged and not stick with a project. However, because of their confidence, they may appear too self-assured at times.

The Monkey gets along well with the Dragon and the Rat. Avoid the Tiger.

THE SIGN OF THE ROOSTER
(sometimes called the chicken)

Roosters interest other people, but they are loners. They are organized and careful in their work, and they love to learn. Full of energy, they are polite and charming. Sometimes, though, they are bossy, causing others to dislike them.

The Rooster gets along well with the Snake and the Ox. Avoid the Rabbit.

THE SIGN OF THE DOG

People born in the time of the Dog are honest, loyal, generous, and intelligent. They are people to be counted on all the time. Dogs dislike chatter and view the world in a simple way. While they pay little attention to money, they always seem to have enough. They sometimes look for trouble where there is none and can be very stubborn.

The Dog gets along well with the Horse and the Tiger. Avoid the Dragon.

THE SIGN OF THE BOAR
(sometimes called the pig)

Those born in the time of the Boar are honorable and noble people. Their family and friends find they are always dedicated, affectionate, and kind. They are also courageous, helpful, and honest. Sometimes they are shy or short-tempered and can be tricked by others less honest.

The Boar gets along best with the Sheep and Rabbit. Avoid other Boars and the Snake.

FINDING YOUR SIGNS

Find out the year, month, day, and hour of your birth, then use these charts to find each sign.

Sign	Hour	Month*	Year
Rat	11:00 p.m. to 1:00 a.m.	December	1900, 1912, 1924, 1936, 1948, 1960, 1972, 1984, 1996
Ox	1:00 a.m. to 3:00 a.m.	January	1901, 1913, 1925, 1937, 1949, 1961, 1973, 1985, 1997
Tiger	3:00 a.m. to 5:00 a.m.	February	1902, 1914, 1926, 1938, 1950, 1962, 1974, 1986, 1998
Rabbit	5:00 a.m. to 7:00 a.m.	March	1903, 1915, 1927, 1939, 1951, 1963, 1975, 1987, 1999
Dragon	7:00 a.m. to 9:00 a.m.	April	1904, 1916, 1928, 1940, 1952, 1964, 1976, 1988, 2000
Snake	9:00 a.m. to 11:00 a.m.	May	1905, 1917, 1929, 1941, 1953, 1965, 1977, 1989, 2001
Horse	11:00 a.m. to 1:00 p.m.	June	1906, 1918, 1930, 1942, 1954, 1966, 1978, 1990, 2002
Sheep	1:00 p.m. to 3:00 p.m.	July	1907, 1919, 1931, 1943, 1955, 1967, 1979, 1991, 2003
Monkey	3:00 p.m. to 5:00 p.m.	August	1908, 1920, 1932, 1944, 1956, 1968, 1980, 1992, 2004
Rooster	5:00 p.m. to 7:00 p.m.	September	1909, 1921, 1933, 1945, 1957, 1969, 1981, 1993, 2005
Dog	7:00 p.m. to 9:00 p.m.	October	1910, 1922, 1934, 1946, 1958, 1970, 1982, 1994, 2006
Boar	9:00 p.m. to 11:00 p.m.	November	1911, 1923, 1935, 1947, 1959, 1971, 1983, 1995, 2007

*Induk assigned these signs to the months. However, these are just approximate because the months of the Chinese calendar change with the cycles of the moon and are different from our calendar's months. So, the month signs actually change from year to year.

TO FIND YOUR DAY SIGN

Step 1. Find on the chart on page 129 the year in which you were born.

Step 2. Look in the second column of this chart to see what the day sign for January 1 is in that year.

Step 3. Find the date with a box around it on the calendar on page 129 that is the nearest one before your birthdate. (If you were born in a leap year—your birth year will have this symbol, "*", next to it on the chart—use the dates after February 28 that have a black box around them.)

Step 4. From that boxed date, count through the birth signs on the chart above in order, starting with the day sign for January 1 of that year.

Step 5. When you reach your birthdate, see what birth sign you're on. That's your day sign.

Example: If you were born on July 4, 1983, look first at the table on page 129 to determine that in 1983, January 1 was a Tiger day. Next, use the calendar to count forward from the nearest boxed date. The closest boxed date before July 4 is June 30. Since all boxed dates are the same sign as January 1 of that year, we know that June 30 is a Tiger day. So starting with the Tiger, count forward through the signs (Rabbit, Dragon, Snake, Horse, etc.) until you get to July 4. You end on Horse. Your day sign, if your birthday is July 4, 1983, is Horse.

The day sign
for January 1
of that year is:

Find the year you were born in:

1930, 1946, 1962, 1978, 1994	Rat
1928*,1937, 1944*, 1953, 1960*, 1969, 1976*, 1985, 1992*	Ox
1935, 1951, 1967, 1983, 1999	Tiger
1926, 1942, 1958, 1974, 1990	Rabbit
1924*, 1933, 1940*, 1949, 1956*, 1965, 1972*, 1981, 1988*, 1997	Dragon
1931, 1947, 1963, 1979, 1995	Snake
1922, 1938, 1954, 1970, 1986	Horse
1929, 1936*, 1945, 1952*, 1961, 1968*, 1977, 1984*, 1993	Sheep
1927, 1943, 1959, 1975, 1991	Monkey
1934, 1950, 1966, 1982, 1998	Rooster
1925, 1932*, 1941, 1948*, 1957, 1964*, 1973, 1980*, 1989, 1996*	Dog
1923, 1939, 1955, 1971, 1987	Boar

*leap year

January

S	M	T	W	T	F	S
1	2	3	4	5	6	7
8	9	10	11	12	13	14
15	16	17	18	19	20	21
22	23	24	25	26	27	28
29	30	31				

February

S	M	T	W	T	F	S
			1	2	3	4
5	6	7	8	9	10	11
12	13	14	15	16	17	18
19	20	21	22	23	24	25
26	27	28	29			

March

S	M	T	W	T	F	S
			1	2	3	4
5	6	7	8	9	10	11
12	13	14	15	16	17	18
19	20	21	22	23	24	25
26	27	28	29	30	31	

April

S	M	T	W	T	F	S
						1
2	3	4	5	6	7	8
9	10	11	12	13	14	15
16	17	18	19	20	21	22
23	24	25	26	27	28	29
30						

May

S	M	T	W	T	F	S
	1	2	3	4	5	6
7	8	9	10	11	12	13
14	15	16	17	18	19	20
21	22	23	24	25	26	27
28	29	30	31			

June

S	M	T	W	T	F	S
				1	2	3
4	5	6	7	8	9	10
11	12	13	14	15	16	17
18	19	20	21	22	23	24
25	26	27	28	29	30	

July

S	M	T	W	T	F	S
						1
2	3	4	5	6	7	8
9	10	11	12	13	14	15
16	17	18	19	20	21	22
23	24	25	26	27	28	29
30	31					

August

S	M	T	W	T	F	S
		1	2	3	4	5
6	7	8	9	10	11	12
13	14	15	16	17	18	19
20	21	22	23	24	25	26
27	28	29	30	31		

September

S	M	T	W	T	F	S
					1	2
3	4	5	6	7	8	9
10	11	12	13	14	15	16
17	18	19	20	21	22	23
24	25	26	27	28	29	30

October

S	M	T	W	T	F	S
1	2	3	4	5	6	7
8	9	10	11	12	13	14
15	16	17	18	19	20	21
22	23	24	25	26	27	28
29	30	31				

November

S	M	T	W	T	F	S
			1	2	3	4
5	6	7	8	9	10	11
12	13	14	15	16	17	18
19	20	21	22	23	24	25
26	27	28	29	30		

December

S	M	T	W	T	F	S
					1	2
3	4	5	6	7	8	9
10	11	12	13	14	15	16
17	18	19	20	21	22	23
24	25	26	27	28	29	30
31						

BIBLIOGRAPHY

Adams, Edward B. *Korea Guide*. Seoul: Seoul International Tourist Publishing Company, 1976.

Chung, Okwha, and Judy Monroe. *Cooking the Korean Way*. Minneapolis: Lerner Publications Company, 1988.

Farley, Carol. *Korea, a Land Divided*. Minneapolis: Dillon Press, Inc., 1983.

Hamlin, Julia. "Zodiac Zoo." *Teen Magazine*, January 1993.

Han, Hyan Sook. *Understanding My Child's Korean Origins*. St. Paul: Children's Home Society of Minnesota, 1980.

Moffett, Eileen F. *Korean Ways*. Seoul: Seoul International Publishing House, 1986.

Pahk, Induk. *The Hour of the Tiger*. New York: Harper and Row, 1965.

Pahk, Induk. *September Monkey*. New York: Harper and Row, 1954.

Trebilcock, Dorothy Warner. "Ewha Women's University: A Voice in the Land of Morning Calm." *Korean Culture*, 9. Los Angeles: Korean Cultural Service, Spring 1988.

Yen, Clara, illustrations by Hideo C. Yoshida. *Why Rat Comes First, A Story of the Chinese Zodiac*. San Francisco: Children's Book Press, 1991.